A COMPLETE GUIDE TO

SPECIAL EFFECTS MAKEUP 3

REALISTIC SCAR MAKEUPS

Gallery 004

A
COMPLETE

SPECIAL EFFECTS MAKEUP 3

GUIDE TO

Chapter01 Complete guide to wound makeup 025

Chapter02

A collection of bloodthirsty serial killers and horror masks 075

o

Chapter03 Modeling and bandages 095

Chapter04 Step-by-step instructions 103

CONTENTS

TOMO HYAKUTAKE
KILLER & TAILOR
PHOTO: YOSUKE KOMATSU
MODEL: SAYAKA MACHI & TENMETSU

SOICHI UMEZAWA
KYUAISHA (ASKING A GIRL OUT)
PHOTO: HIRONOBU ONODERA
MODEL: SHIGERU OKUSE

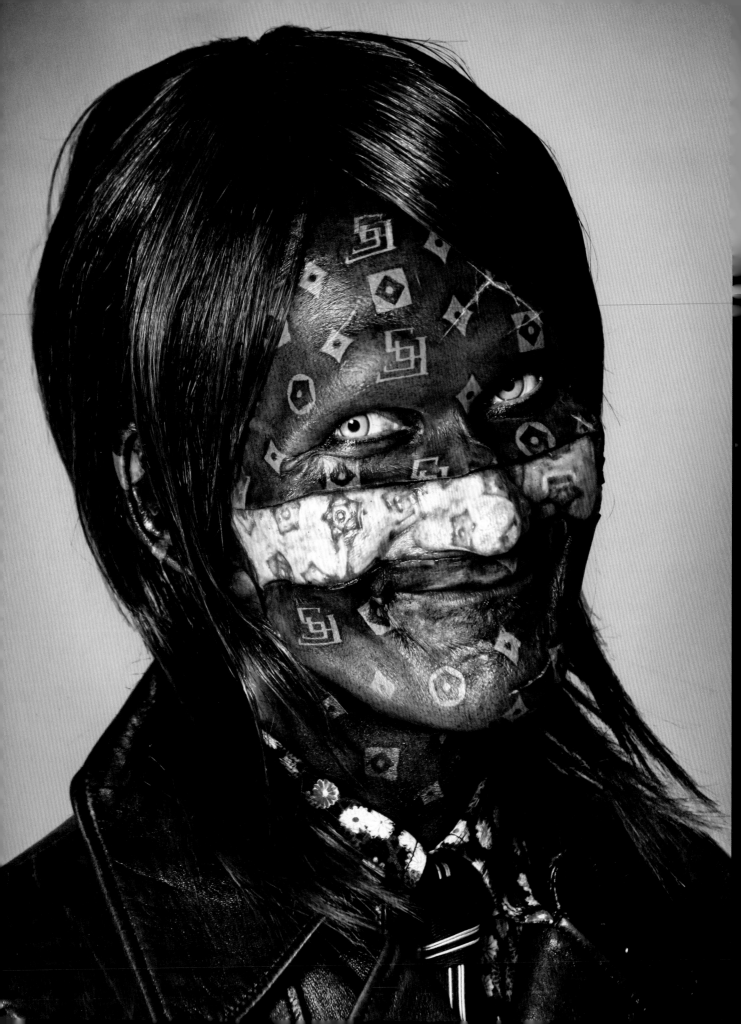

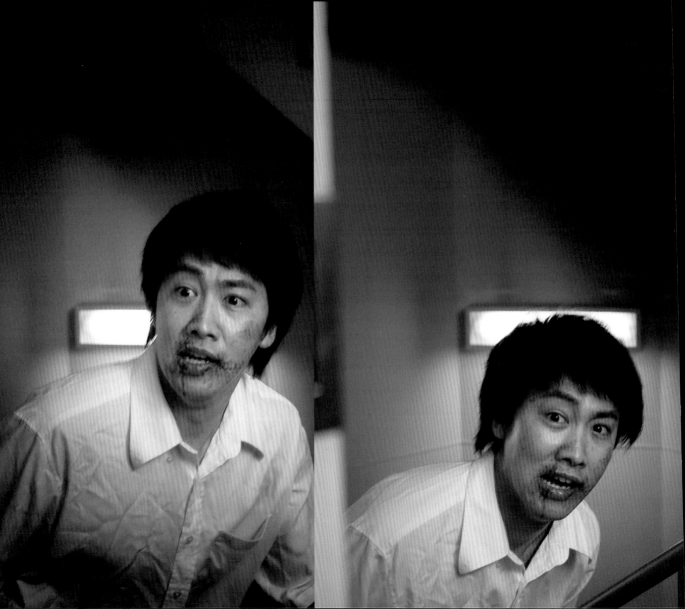

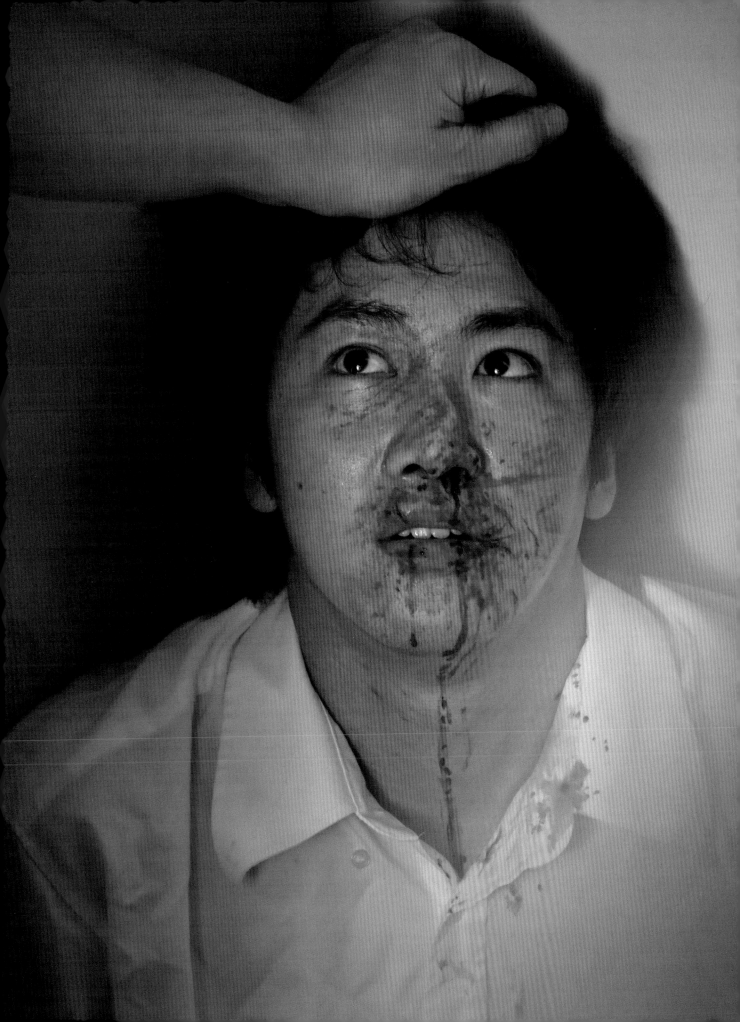

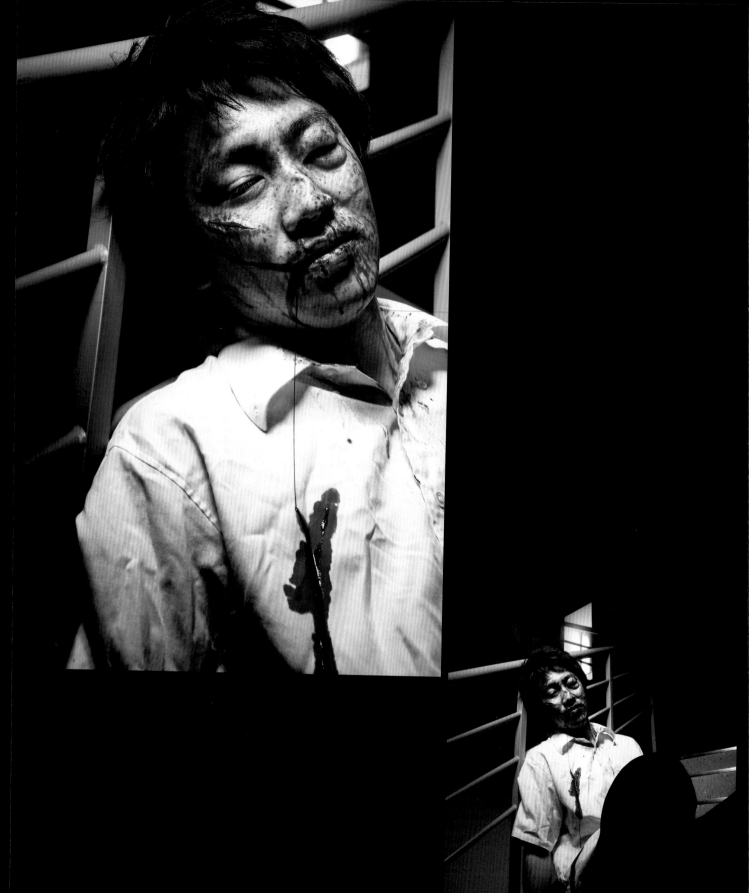

TOMONOBU IWAKURA
KOGEKI (ASSAULT)
PHOTO: HIRONOBU ONODERA
MODEL: HIROAKI MURAKAMI

KAKUSEI FUJIWARA
MORGUE BRIDE

PHOTO: MASASHI NAGAO
MODEL: AYA

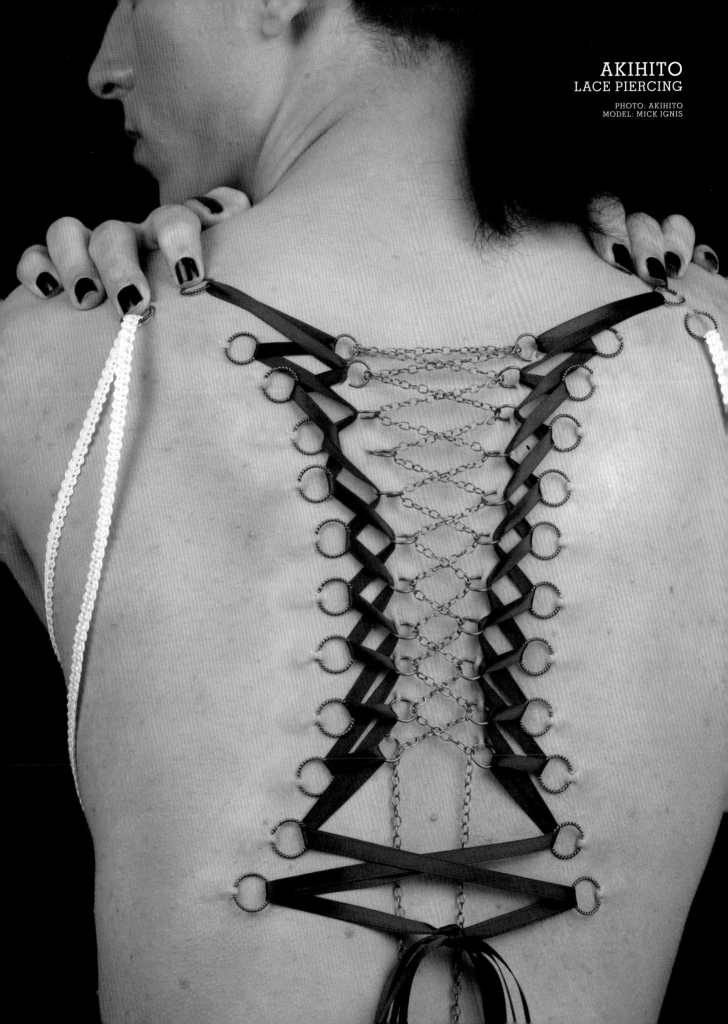

AKIHITO
LACE PIERCING
PHOTO: AKIHITO
MODEL: MICK IGNIS

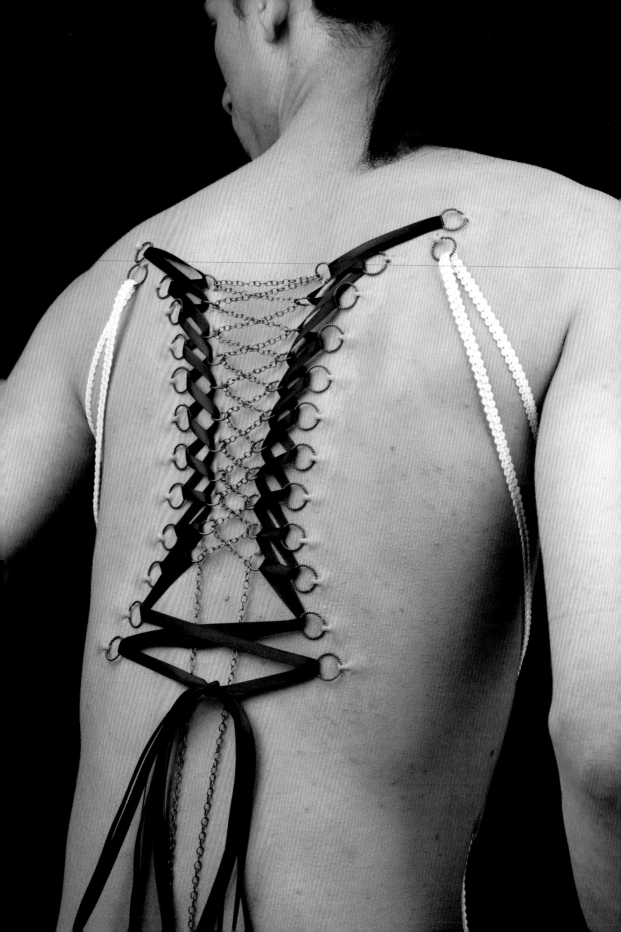

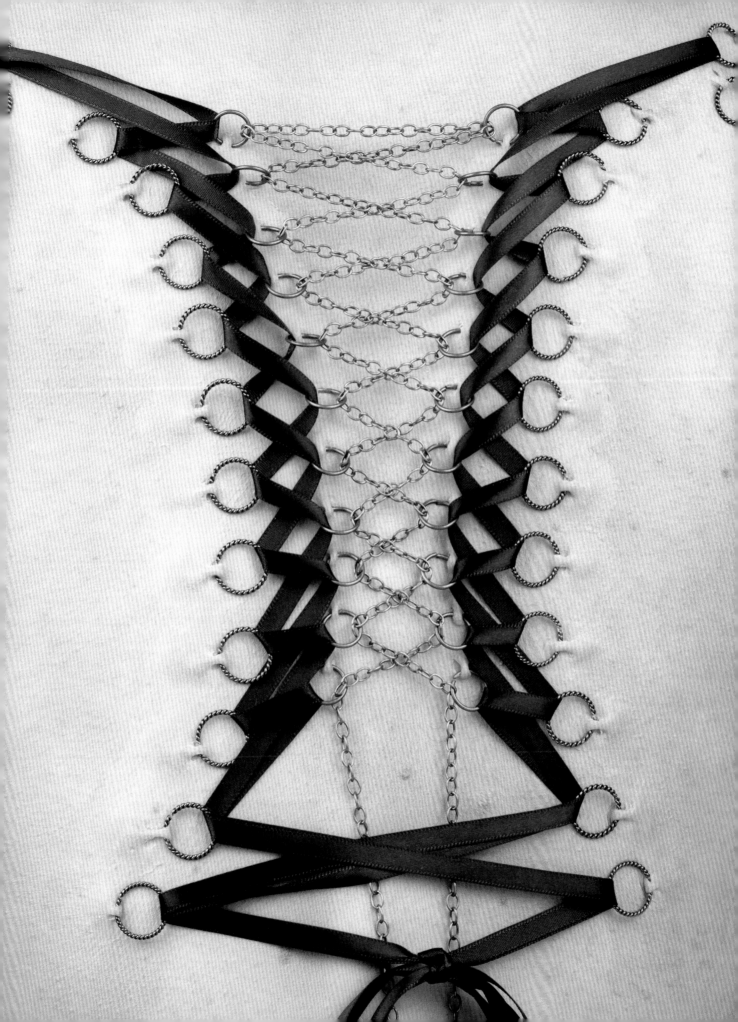

MAKIKO KONO
TRICK OR TREAT
PHOTO: YOSUKE KOMATSU
MODEL: MAKIKO

 First Place Prize: Wound Makeup Contest

CHIE ICHIGAYA

NINGYO (Doll)

Concept: Mending a torn doll

Materials: 3rd degree silicone modeling compound, grease paints, thread, cotton

School Studied/Studying: AMAZING SCHOOL JUR

■ **Takashi Shimizu (Film Director)**
First of all, this contestant took a unique approach to creating wound makeup. I like the fact that she used blood in a subtle and effective way. The composition of the photograph is nice and not too "made up."

■ **Yoshihiro Nishimura (Film Director)**
This makeup uses a two-part silicone mix. The most common mistake in using two-part silicone is applying too much and overdoing the makeup. However, this work is very delicate. I don't know if it was done on purpose or not, but I loved the use of cotton balls on the neck combined with the overall delicate feel of the makeup. Also – from looking at the photograph – I can tell that the contestant had a certain vision while she was working on this piece. As far as the sense of color goes, she deliberately chose a greenish tone for the photograph to make the color of the blood appear more dark. Taking all of the above into consideration, I have humbly chosen this work for the first place prize.

■ **Yudai Yamaguchi (Film Director)**
Regardless of how well special effects makeup is done, it has to be photographed well in order to properly showcase the work. This piece is truly superior because of the quality of the photograph and the technical aspects of the special effects makeup.

WOUND
makeup

COMPLETE GUIDE TO WOUND MAKEUP

WOUND 01

Scrapes

by Akiteru Nakada

Scrapes that would result from grating your skin across asphalt. It should only take about ten minutes to produce these scrapes using paint. The chosen material for this makeup is Liquitex, a paint that remains on the skin once it dries. When compared to stage blood, Liquitex comes in very handy because of its water-resistant properties.

[Materials]
Liquitex (Quinacridone red orange, ivory black, purple)
[Tools]
Kitchen sponge, fine-tip brush

Model: Hanako

02
Mix Liquitex ivory black in Quinacridone red orange so that it has a similar color to blood. The key is to make it a bit darker than you would think.

02
Spread the mixed paint on your hand, and take up some color with a kitchen sponge. Gently rub the sponge against your model's skin.

03
Add thick lines to represent scrapes and blood by brushing on lines with the same color.

04
If the surrounding skin looks too clean, the wounds will appear fake. So, rub purple Liquitex on the surrounding skin to create a bruised look.

05
Leave some natural skin color around the scrapes to act as highlights. This will give the scrapes a more realistic appearance.

06
Add black streaks in the middle of the scrapes. This creates depth and sharpness.

07
Complete.

WOUND
makeup

Slit Mouth

by Kakusei Fujiwara

This is a slit wound where the corner of the mouth has been cut with scissors. Apply Cabosil mixed with Pros-Aide to create the slit and then apply makeup. It should take about fifteen minutes to complete this wound!

Cabosil mixed with Pros-Aide is a material for special effects makeup that uses the medical adhesive Pros-Aide and special fumed silica called Cabosil.

[Materials]
Cabosil mixed in Pros-Aide, Dura (skin tone, red), Skin Illustrator (red), stage blood
[Tools]
Spatula, brushes, orange stipple sponge

Model: Hanako

01 Apply Cabosil, mixed with Pros-Aide, in the shape of a slit using a spatula.

02 Use a sponge to add a coarse texture to the slit.

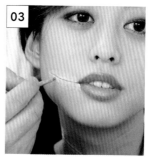

03 Apply skin toned Dura over the area where the Cabosil/Pros-Aide was applied.

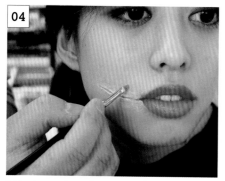

04 Add redness using red colored Dura.

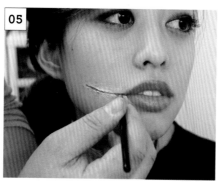

05 Paint the inside of the slit using red Skin Illustrator.

06 Take some red Skin Illustrator on an orange stipple sponge and dab the surrounding skin.

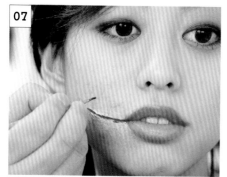

07 Draw capillary vessels using red Skin Illustrator.

08 Apply stage blood inside the slit.

COMPLETE! Turn your model's face upward and add some stage blood drops to complete!

Whipping Wound

by Soichi Umezawa

This is a wound caused by a single strike from a powerful lash of bamboo or leather. Glue a piece of cotton on the skin using liquid latex and apply paint to produce an open wound. Liquid latex is a product commonly used for prosthetic makeup. It can also act as glue.

[Materials]
Liquid latex, eyeliner, cotton balls, Liquitex (red, blue), grease paint (skin tone), stage blood, acrylic paint (red)
[Tools]
Spatula, sponge, toothbrush, hair dryer

01 Sketch the outline of the wound using eyeliner. Then, apply liquid latex over the sketch using a sponge.

02 Take a small shred of cotton and lay it down on the wet liquid latex. The liquid latex acts as glue.

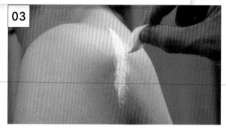
03 Apply another layer of liquid latex over the cotton. Then lay another shred of cotton on the wet liquid latex. Blow dry. This will create a "ripped skin" texture.

04 Peel off some latex to give the appearance of split flesh.

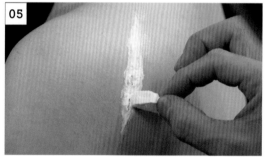
05 Once again apply a layer of liquid latex. Blow dry and then carve some more wounds. Repeat this until you achieve the desired image. Just be careful not to overdo things.

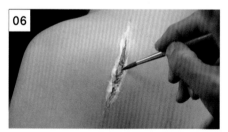
06 Mix Liquitex red and blue to create a reddish purple color. Apply that to the inside of the wound.

07 Apply liquid latex. Apply skin tone grease paint along the outer edges of the wound.

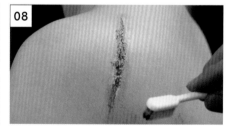
08 Use a toothbrush to rub stage blood inside the wound to create a scrape-like look.

09 Apply red acrylic paint to deepen the wound and add shadows.

COMPLETE! Splatter some stage blood on the wound using a toothbrush to add small bloody spots. Apply stage blood inside the wound to complete!

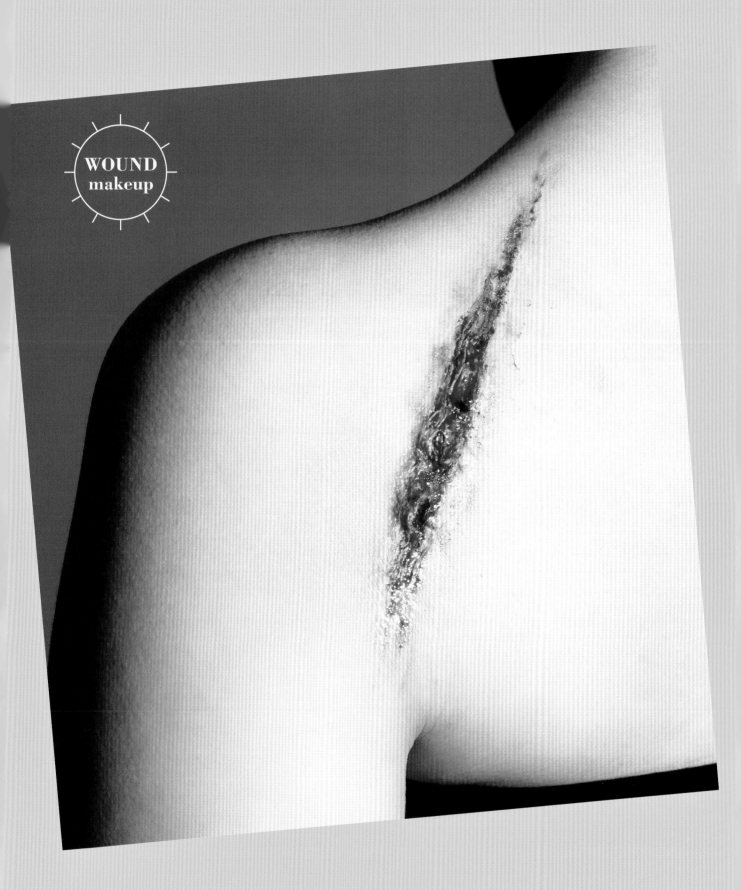

WOUND
makeup

Choking Bruises

by Akiteru Nakada

These bruises around the neck are a result of severe choking with a single hand. Repeated application of paint and then powder creates bruises.

[Materials]
Grease paint (red, blue, yellow, green), loose setting powder
[Tools]
Fine-tip brush, powder puff

Model: Hanako

01 Sketch bruises using red grease paint. Draw four finger shapes to show where severe pressure was applied and caused bruising.

02 Make the area around the adam's apple intensely red.

03 Smudge the redness with your fingertips.

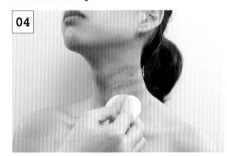

04 Apply loose setting powder.

05 Do not paint evenly because bruises are made up of uneven hemorrhaging! Leave the unevenness of the color, while remembering the plasticity of the neck.

06 Draw veins using a fine-tipped brush.

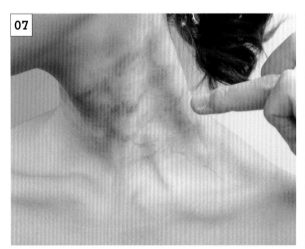

07 Apply yellow-green grease paint with your fingertips between the bruises. Aim to create a look where the capillaries are visible under the yellowish skin.

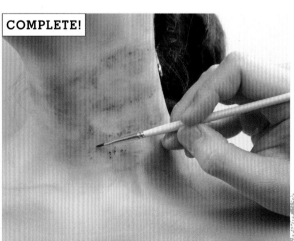

COMPLETE! Add purple grease paint on the bruises and then smudge with your fingertip. Add red dots to produce the look of damaged capillary vessels. Do not add too much! Apply loose setting powder to blend.

Rope Marks

by Kakusei Fujiwara

Use Rigid Collodion to produce dents on the skin that were caused by rope. Rigid Collodion is a water-resistant liquid used as a medical topical protectant. It is used to close small wounds. This makeup should take ten minutes to complete.

[Materials]
Rigid Collodion, Pros-Aide, loose setting powder, liquid paint (e.g. acrylic)
[Tools]
Brushes, sponge

Model: Hanako

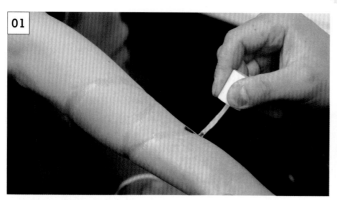

01

Apply Rigid Collodion to the areas where you want to produce rope marks.

02

Let dry for a short time. When Rigid Collodion completely dries it will pull the skin tight. Do not let it dry too much.

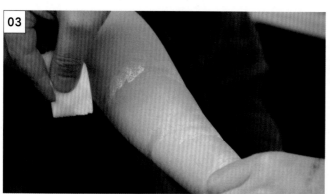

03

Rigid Collodion will peel off easily, so apply some Pros-Aide using a sponge to keep that from happening.

04

Over the Pros-Aide, add redness using liquid-based paint.

COMPLETE!

Apply loose setting powder to complete!

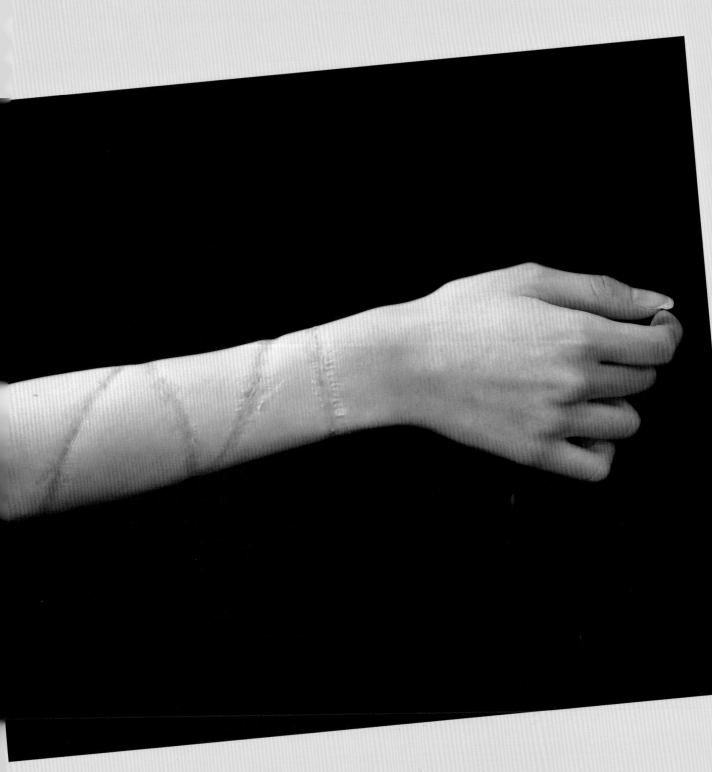

WOUND
makeup

Stab Wound

by Tomo Hyakutake

This stab wound is caused by a paring knife or a butterfly knife. The flesh has been pierced all the way to the heel of the blade. Use Oblaat (a thin transparent edible sheet made from algae and starch) to make the wound look realistic.

[Materials]
Oblaat, Skin Illustrator (red, blue), ethanol, acrylic paint, stage blood, TELESIS

[Tools]
Cotton swabs, brushes

01 Fold a sheet of oblaat and then roll it up. Apply TELESIS where you want the wound to be. Then lay the rolled oblaat in the shape of a wound.

02 Flatten the oblaat using a brush.

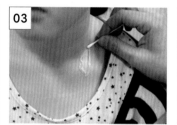

03 Adjust the shape of the wound with a cotton swab.

04 Wet another sheet of oblaat and make a small ball. Stick the oblaat ball inside the wound and flatten using a cotton swab.

05 Paint the outer edge of the wound using red Skin Illustrator.

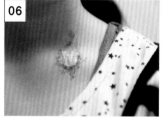

06 Thin out some ethanol and then drop in some acrylic paint to make a watery red-purple. Use that to produce the redness around the outer edges of the wound.

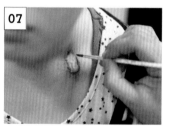

07 Trace the outer edge of the wound with red Skin Illustrator. Then add some red dots.

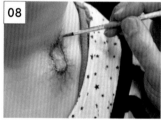

08 Add dots using blue Skin Illustrator. Draw blood vessels using the red-purple you used in step 04.

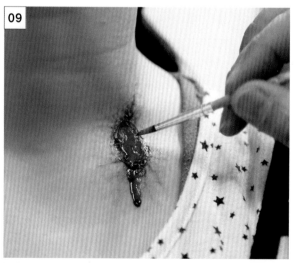

09 Apply stage blood inside the wound and also apply some stage blood unevenly outside of the wound.

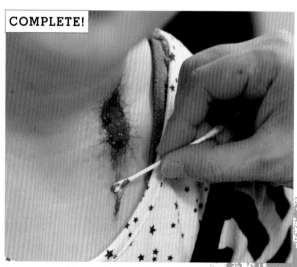

COMPLETE! Adjust the stage blood on the wound using a wet cotton swab based on the image you have in your mind. Complete.

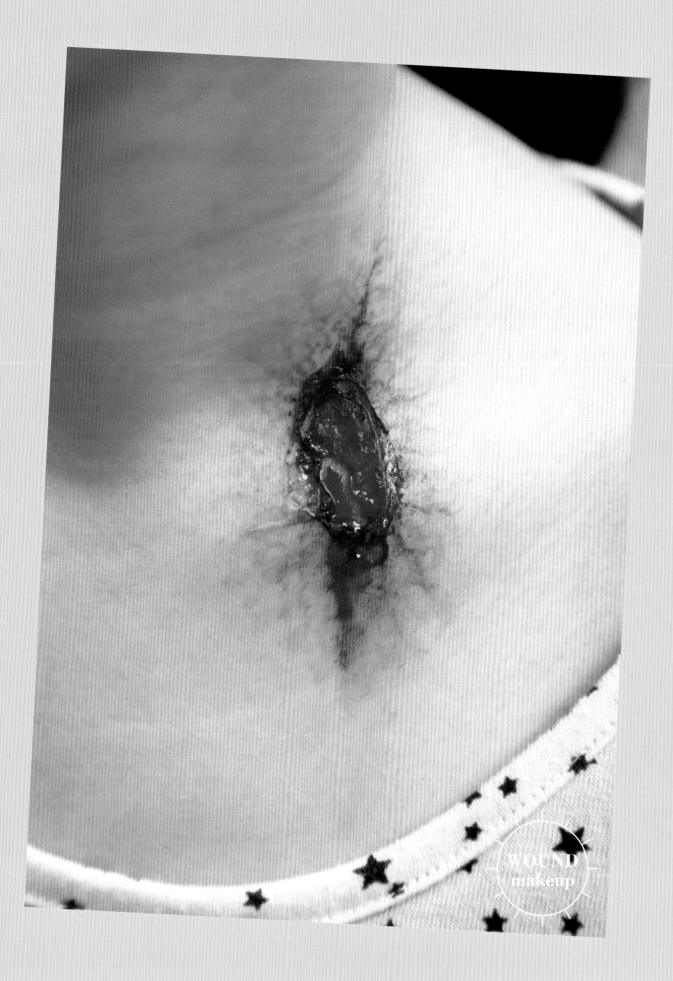

Slit on the Neck

by Kakusei Fujiwara

This gash on the neck is caused by a large knife. Arteries are deep under the skin, so this particular example uses *nori no tsukudani* (laver boiled down in soy sauce) in order to give depth to the wound. *Nori no tsukudani* can be substituted with squid ink, which produces a similar effect. If you wish to achieve the texture produced in this example, it is recommended that you use *nori no tsukudani*. It should be available at most Asian food markets or online. Platsil Gel 10 is used to produce wounded skin and fake skin.

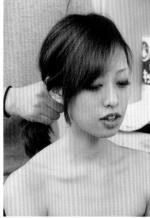

[Materials]
Eyeliner, Platsil Gel 10 (three parts part A, three parts part B, one part deadener), grease paint (red), Super Baldiez, stage blood, *nori no tsukudani* (or squid ink)
[Tools]
Spatula, sponge

Model: Hanako

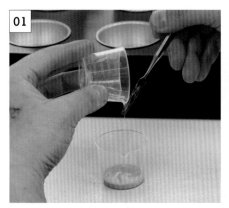

01

Mix equal parts of Platsil Gel 10 part A and part B, and one-third the amount of deadener.

02

Plot out the shape of the wound using eyeliner.

03

Apply the Gel 10 around the plotted line.

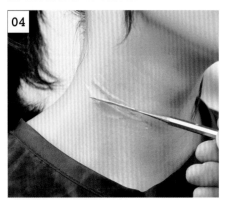

04

Smooth out the application using a spatula.

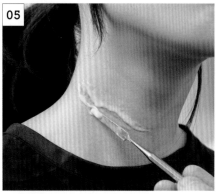

05

Apply another layer of the Gel 10 mixture.

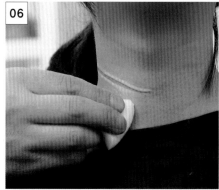

06

Smooth out the application using a sponge.

07

Apply red grease paint to the inside of the wound.

08

Apply a layer of Super Baldiez (a material that produces a thin film and acts as a glue) over the wound. Then add drops of stage blood.

COMPLETE!

Apply *nori no tsukudani* or squid ink on the wound to complete.

Old Scars

by Akiteru Nakada

Use a liquid bandage to produce scars from an old wound.

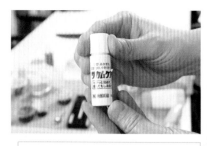

[Materials]
Liquid bandage (works similarly to rigid collodion), grease paint (red, blue, purple, brown)

[Tools]
Brushes, spatula, hair dryer

Model: Hanako

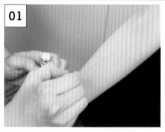

01 Apply liquid bandage in the shape of a scar.

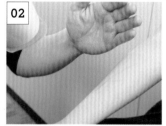

02 Blow dry. As it dries the skin will tighten.

03 Apply another coat of liquid bandage.

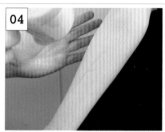

04 Blow dry again.

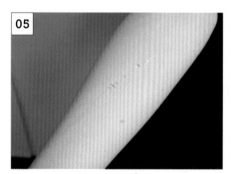

05 The photo above shows where the skin has tightened after the liquid bandage dried.

06 Mix red, brown, and purple grease paint and then apply the mixture to the inside of the scar. Remember, every scar is different. Some are pinkish while others are brownish. So be sure to produce your chosen color according to your intentions.

07 Mix red and brown grease paint and lay it down around the scar. Then smudge the grease paint with your fingertip. Add some partial emphasis.

08 Apply bluish-purple grease paint to blend the edges of the scar.

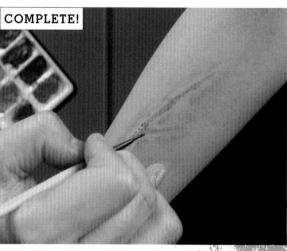

COMPLETE! Lightly add some intense red to the scar to complete!

WOUND
makeup

Bruised Face and Swollen Black Eye

by Soichi Umezawa

This makeup will produce a realistic swollen and bruised face. This trauma was caused by repeated punches to the side of the eye and mouth. To create a swollen eyelid, use Eye Putti or eyelid glue and hold the eyelid down. Put some cotton balls inside your model's mouth to reproduce the realistic look of a swollen cheek.

[Materials]
Eye Putti or eyelid glue, face paint (red, purple), grease paint (red, brown, blue, green, black), cotton ball
[Tools]
Spatula, sponge, brushes, hair dryer

Model: Aya

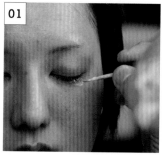

01

Apply Eye Putti or eyelid glue on the upper and lower eyelids to hold them together.

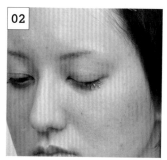

02

Blow dry the Eye Putti or eyelid glue. Repeat this until the chosen eye is shut.

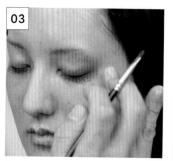

03

Use face paint to add reddish-purple shadows around the socket of the closed eye.

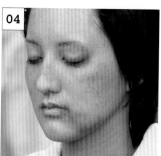

04

Add redness to the side of the mouth and nose.

05

Mix brown, blue, green, and black grease paint to create a dark color. Apply the mixed color from one corner of the eye to the other.

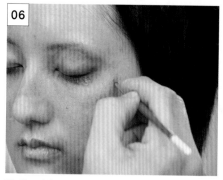

06

Starting at the temple, apply red-purple face paint in a circular motion along the cheekbone.

07

Mix red and brown grease paint and apply the mixture thickly over the cheekbone. The area where the bone protrudes has a more intense redness because the blood vessels underneath the skin are prone to damage from impact.

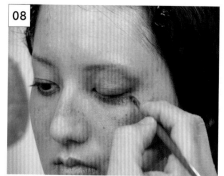

08

While gauging the overall balance, darken the outer corner of the eye. Mix red and blue grease paint and add that to the middle of the forehead.

09

Add red dots using grease paint inside the reddish bruises. Draw the blood vessels. Below the mouth, apply some red for blood.

COMPLETE!

Put some cotton balls inside of your model's mouth to complete!

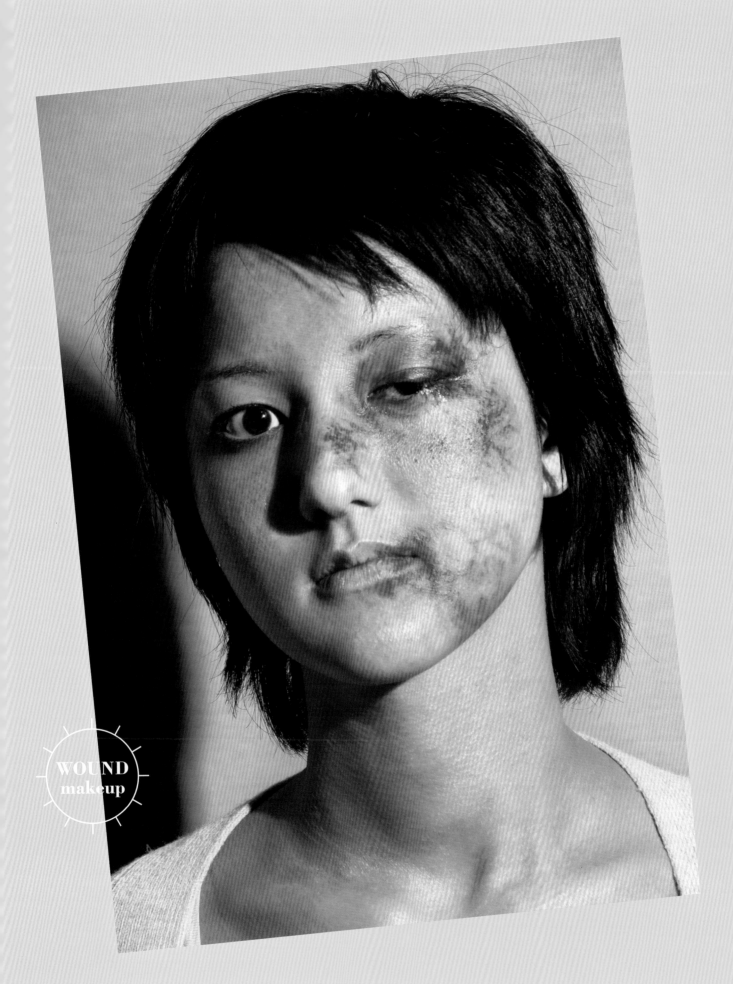

WOUND
makeup

Gunshot Wound

by Akiteru Nakada

This is a gunshot wound to the forehead. All you need is paint for this makeup. Usually, an entry wound is small, as seen in this makeup. However, an exit wound (in this case at the back of the head) would cause more serious damage.

[Materials]
Grease paint (black, red, brown, purple, white), Liquitex (red)

[Tools]
Fine-tip brush

Model: Hanako

01

Draw a circle for the entry wound using grease paint.

02

Draw punctured skin as if the gunshot was made while the muzzle of a gun was touching the forehead. When gunshots are made from a distance you won't see this type of puncture wound.

03

Fill the opening of the wound with black.

04

Add white highlights (to create the swelling of the flesh).

05

Apply white for the bone.

06

Add shadows to produce the look of swollen flesh.

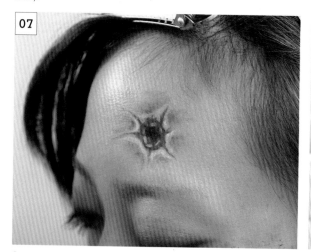

07

Smudge the shadow using your finger.

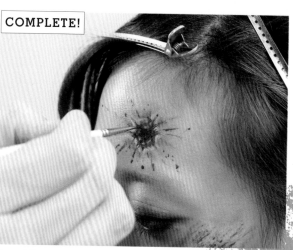

COMPLETE!

Use red Liquitex to paint blood spatter around the wound to complete!

WOUND
makeup

Stitched Wound

by Tomo Hyakutake

The corner of the mouth is slit open and then stitched up. Apply silicone putty around the painted wound, then glue down short strands of thread for each stitch.

Model: Aya

[Materials]
Grease paint (black, brown, red, blue), 3rd Degree (silicone modeling compound), thread, Pros-Aide, liquid latex

[Tools]
Spatula, brushes, tweezers, cotton swabs, hair dryer

01 — Mix black and brown grease paint to create a dark brown. This will be used to plot where you want the wound to be. The rule of thumb is to connect the wound and the corner of the mouth.

02 — Trace the lines of the wound using red grease paint.

03 — Draw jagged skin using black grease paint.

04 — Mix 3rd Degree part A and part B, then apply to each side of the wound.

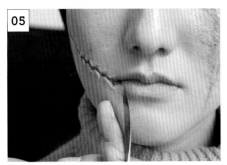
05 — Smooth it out using a spatula.

06 — Prepare short strands of thread for each stitch in advance. Apply liquid latex on each end of the strand and then place on a film sheet.

07 — Pick up each thread using tweezers and apply Pros-Aide on to the ends.

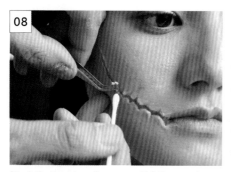

08 Attach the threads so they cross-stitch the wound.

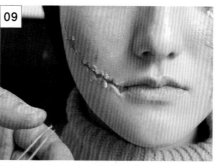

09 The photo above shows the model after all the threads have been attached.

10 Blow dry.

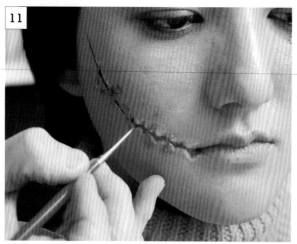

11 Apply black grease paint to the edge of the wound.

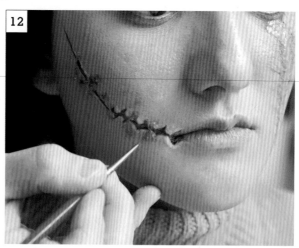

12 Apply some dark brown around the wound.

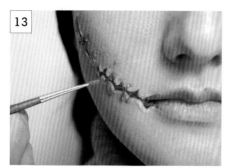

13 Mix some red and brown grease paint, then apply the mixture around the base of each stitch.

14 Apply thinned stage blood inside the wound.

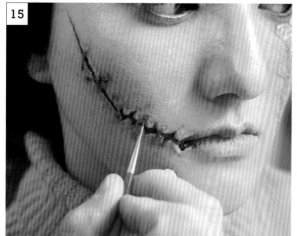

15 Apply reddish purple to make the skin around the wound appear dirty.

COMPLETE! Complete!

Deep, Open Wound Created by a Hatchet

by Akiteru Nakada

This is a deep open wound caused by a hatchet. We use edible gelatin powder to produce damaged flesh.

Model: Hanako

[Materials]
Edible gelatin powder, food dye, eyeliner, alcohol, paint (skin tone, red), grease paint (red, black), loose setting powder

[Tools]
Syringes, small container (to hold warm water), spatula

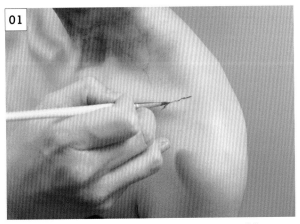

01 Use grease paint to plot out a deep open wound from your model's shoulder to his or her chest. Extending the wound to the shoulder brings out depth and plasticity, thus creating a realistic look.

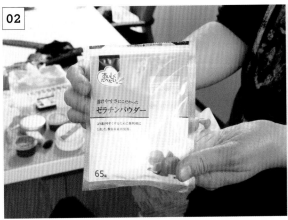

02 Dissolve edible gelatin powder in warm water. Add skin color and red paint to the gelatin. Pour the mixture into a syringe. Pour warm water into a small container and put the filled syringes in water to prevent the gelatin from solidifying.

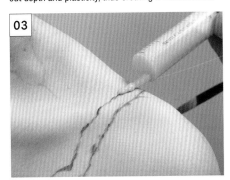

03 Dispense the gelatin mixture from the syringe along the line you plotted.

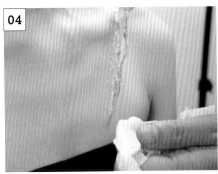

04 Smooth out the gelatin mixture using a spatula. This completes one side of the wound.

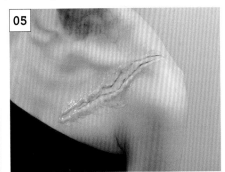

05 Do the same for the other side of the wound.

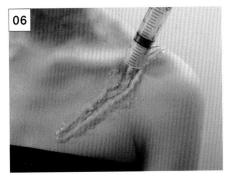

06 Dispense the gelatin mixture thinly inside the wound to produce flesh.

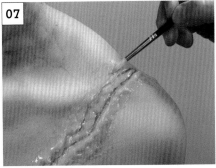

07 Use alcohol to smooth out the edges of the gelatin mixture.

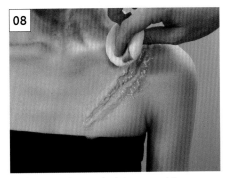

08 Apply loose setting powder to remove moisture.

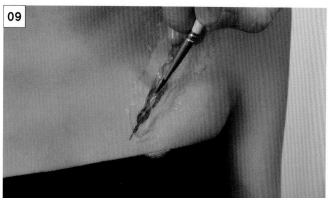

Apply red grease paint unevenly inside the wound.

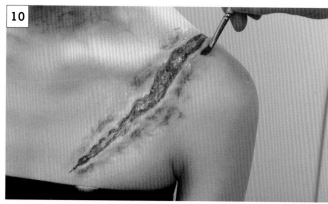

Add brown shadows around the wound.

Smudge the shadows using your fingertip.

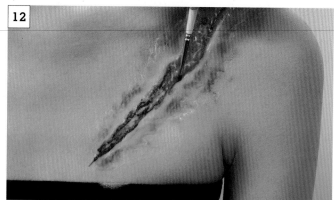

Trace the inside edges of the wound with black grease paint to bring out depth.

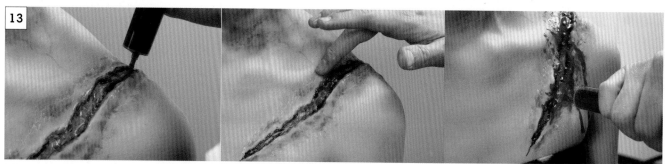

Add more gelatin mixture inside the wound by dispensing from the syringe.

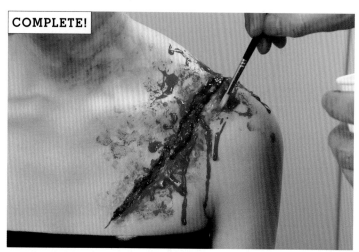

Add black grease paint to the edges of the wound.

WOUND
makeup

Self-inflicted Cuts

by Tomo Hyakutake

Use oblaat and foam material glue to produce cuts on the wrist. For demonstration purposes this sample is slightly overdone. Feel free to decrease the number of cuts or make the color paler based on the image in your mind.

[Materials]
Oblaat, foam material glue, water, Dura (skin tone), grease paint (red, skin tone, blue, orange)
[Tools]
Brushes, cotton swabs

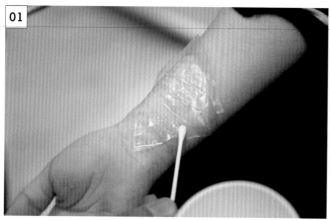

01

Apply foam material glue in the shape of cuts on a sheet of oblaat. Apply that sheet of oblaat to the skin of your model. With the glue side facing up, place the cuts on the inside of the forearm after wetting. Use a cotton swab to push the oblaat sheet so it sticks to the skin.

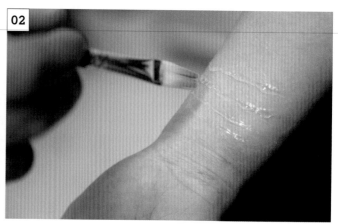

02

Rub the bristles of a wet brush against the oblaat sheet so it sticks to the skin.

03

The photo above shows the oblaat after it was glued down.

04

Make another oblaat sheet of foam material glue as in step 1. Repeat the steps above to glue it to the skin.

05

Apply skin tone Dura on the forearm.

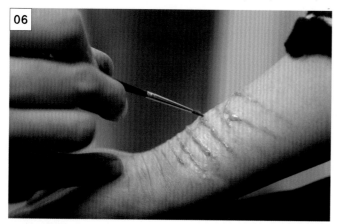

06

Mix red, skin tone, blue, and orange grease paint. Apply paint to each cut to bring out depth.

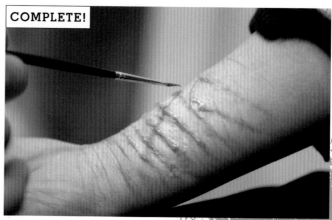

COMPLETE!

Add redness to complete!

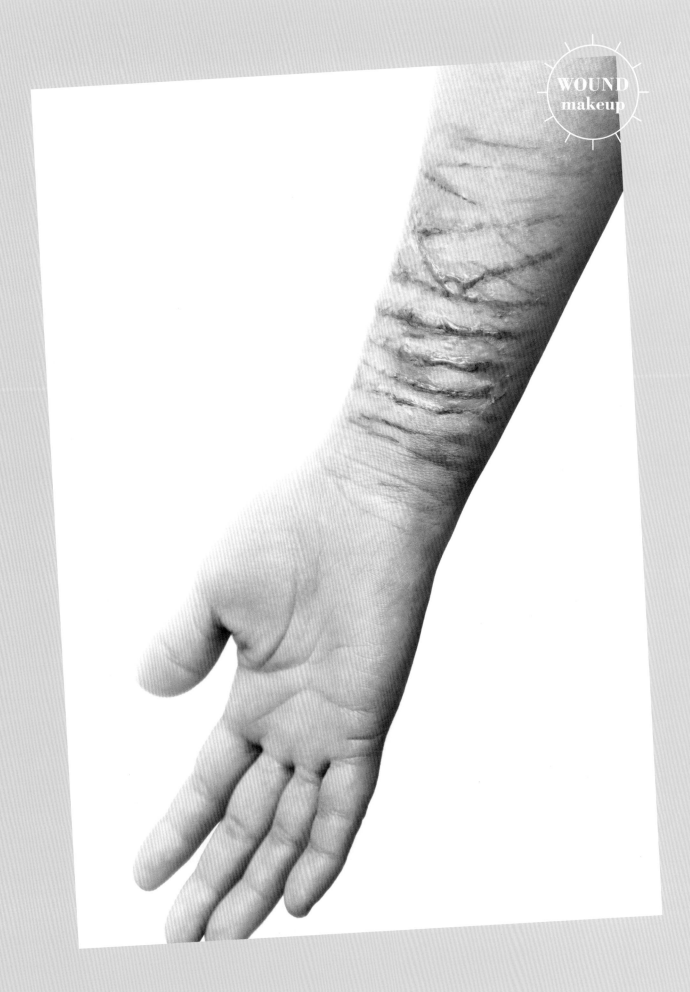

WOUND
makeup

Deep Gash - Chainsaw Wound

by Kakusei Fujiwara

This is a gory wound that a chainsaw gouged out of flesh. The gash is large, so use jute cord and other materials to create a heavily textured wound.

Model: Hanako

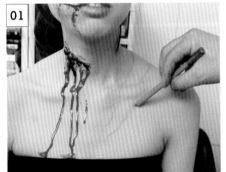

[Materials]
Eyeliner, tissue paper, jute cord, Pros-Aide (medial adhesive), water-soluble putty (can be substituted with Cabosil mixed Pros-Aide), Skin Illustrator (red, blue, yellow, brown), stage blood, black sesame paste

[Tools]
Brushes, cotton swabs, sponge, spray bottle

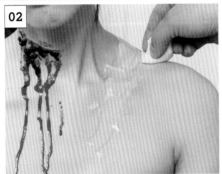

01

Use eyeliner to plot the shape of the wound.

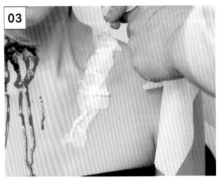

02

Apply Pros-Aide over the area of the wound.

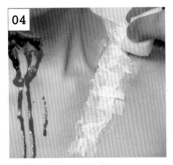

03

Tear tissue paper into jagged pieces and then lay those pieces over the wound.

04

Dab Pros-Aide over the tissue paper.

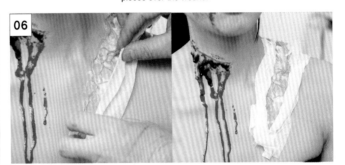

05

Unwind a piece of jute cord and lay it down on the Pros-Aide. Make the jute cord look like the fibers of a piece of flesh.

06

Fold tissue paper and lay it down so it encases the wound. This creates the flesh surrounding the gash.

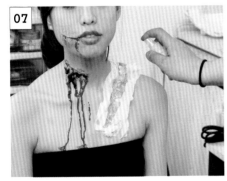

07

Spray with water.

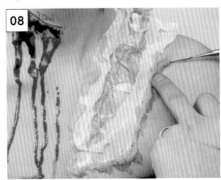

08

Apply water-soluble putty along the edges of the tissue paper.

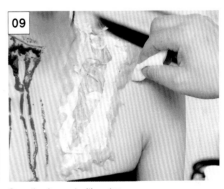

09

Smooth edges out with water.

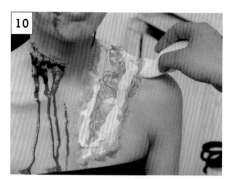

Dab Pros-Aide over the edges of the wound, including the tissue paper and the putty.

Paint the inside of the wound with red Skin Illustrator.

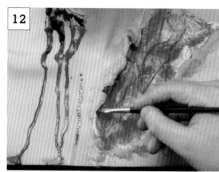

Paint the edges of the wound using blue Skin Illustrator.

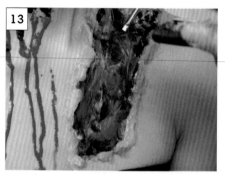

Mix red and blue Skin Illustrator to make purple. Then, apply that to partially illustrate the color of the flesh where the damage is worst.

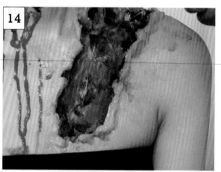

Apply yellow on the edges of the wound to make it look dirty.

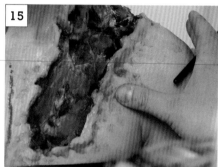

Unevenly smudge yellow shades of color to the surrounding area using your fingertip.

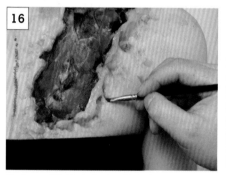

Use brown Skin Illustrator to add shadows where the wound bulges out.

Add black sesame paste or squid ink.

Apply stage blood and then spray water on the blood.

COMPLETE!

Ripped Off Nail

by Soichi Umezawa

Create fake skin over the nail to produce a finger that has had the nail ripped off. Use double-sided tape to produce the flesh under the nail and the nail tip. We use both the thick and the thin type of double-sided tape.

[Materials]
Double-sided tape (thin-type, thick-type), grease paint (skin tone, red, brown), stage blood, false nail, castor oil

[Tools]
Toothpicks, scissors, spatula

Model: Aya

01 Cut thin-type double-sided tape to a length that is a little longer than the chosen nail. Trim off the corners of the double-sided tape.

02 Wrap the double-sided tape around the tip of the nail.

03 Press the surface of the double-sided tape down using a spatula. This will create flesh unevenness where the nail is ripped off.

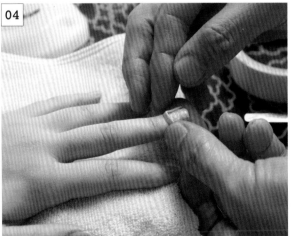

04 Use thick double-sided tape to encase the nail and create the flesh surrounding the nail.

05 Cut thick double-sided tape in a circular shape and then paste that on the nail.

06 Use thin double-sided tape to level off the surrounding flesh and the nail. Use a toothpick to achieve a clean finish.

Apply skin toned grease paint over and around the nail.

Mix red and brown grease paint. Apply along the edges of the nail.

Apply reddish brown around the nail to create a bloody look.

Mix castor oil with red, brown, and blue grease paint. Apply to create a bloody look.

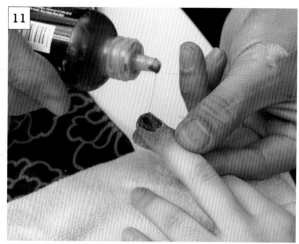

Drop stage blood on the nail.

Adjust the overall shape using a toothpick.

Drip some stage blood and then brush to create unevenness. Repeat until you reach the intended effect.

Cut the false nail similar to your model's nail shape.

Paint red grease paint on the back of the false nail.

Drop some stage blood on the false nail to create a bloody look. Place that on your model's finger so it looks like the nail has been ripped off.

Scar Running Across the Eye

by Tomo Hyakutake

This is an old scar caused by a knife slashing from forehead to cheek. Use woodworking adhesive to produce fake skin. This creates the look of an old wound where the gash was so wide it left a significant scar.

[Materials]
Dura (red, red-purple), Pros-Aide, woodworking adhesive
[Tools]
Plastic board, brushes, spatula

Model: Aya

01 Pour some woodworking adhesive on the surface of a sticker sheet and then work on it to make the shape of your scar. Leave it to dry. Adjust the size of the scar according to your model's face.

02 From the backside of the scar, apply red Dura to produce an aged look.

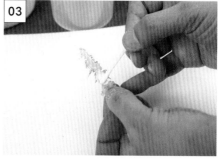

03 Apply Pros-Aide on the backside of the scar, then leave it dry. Paste the scar on your model's face below the eye.

04 For the scar above the eyebrow, repeat the steps above to create a prosthetic scar. Apply the prosthetic over on your model's face above the eyebrow.

05 Apply red-purple Dura around the scars and blend in with the skin.

06 Apply soft-type woodworking adhesive to fill the gap between the scars.

07 In a dotting motion, lay down some skin toned color so you create the appearance of healed skin.

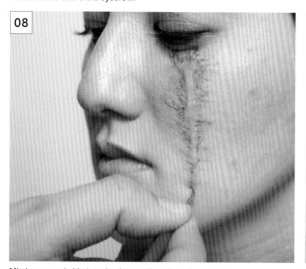

08 Mix brown and skin toned colors, and apply to the edge the scar.

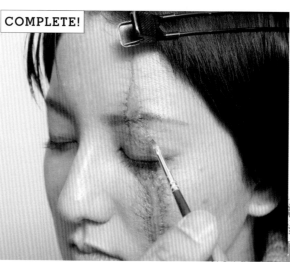

COMPLETE! Add some yellow on the eyelid to complete! As time passes, the woodworking adhesive will stiffen. Once your prosthetic is ready, apply additional makeup as soon as possible.

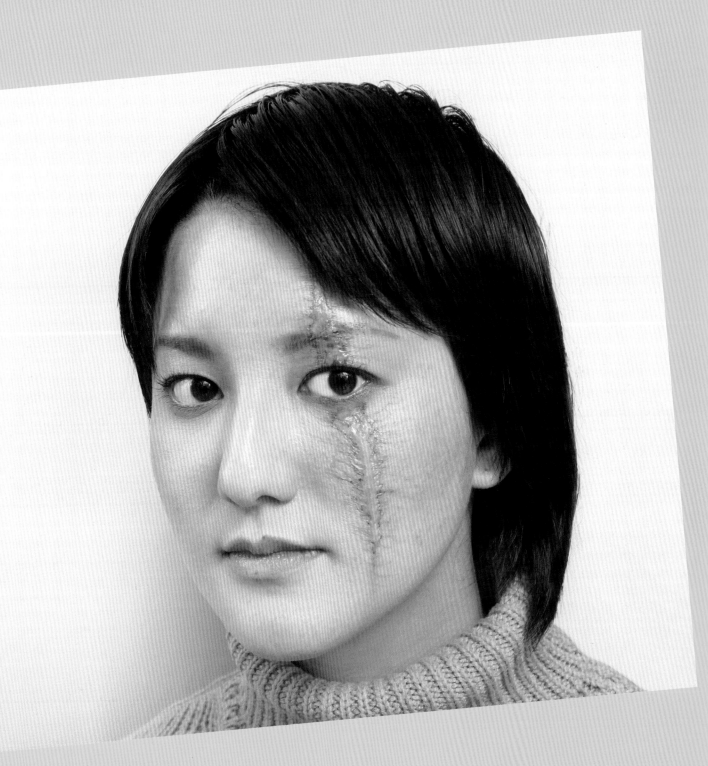

WOUND
makeup

Blisters from an Infectious Disease

[Materials]
Bubble wrap (small, large), Eye Putti or eyelid glue, acrylic paint (white, red, blue), grease paint (white, brown, blue), face paint (red, purple, black, brown)

[Tools]
Scissors, brushes, cotton swabs, lighter, hair dryer

Model: Aya

by Soichi Umezawa

Use different sizes of bubble wrap to create blisters from an unknown infectious disease. Use Eye Putti or eyelid glue to attach the bubble wrap. Make the area around the eyes red to create a feverish look.

01

Cut off a single bubble from a sheet of large bubble wrap.

02

Pass the bubble over a lighter to make it firm and tight. Be careful not to pierce it. Even a tiny hole will make the bubble deflate.

03

Apply Eye Putti or eyelid glue on the backside of the bubble.

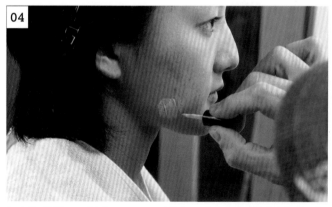

04

Apply Eye Putti or eyelid glue on your model's face where the bubble is to be glued. Blow dry the glue to create a base.

05

Glue the bubble on the base.

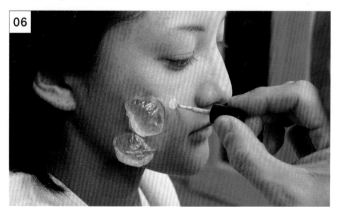

06

Repeat the steps above to glue on more bubbles.

07

In order to produce "the feel of a rapid outbreak of blisters," glue small bubbles around the large blisters.

08 Glue less bubbles on the left side because the idea is that the right side is the source of the outbreak. It looks more realistic if both sides don't appear similar.

09 Glue a small bubble in the middle of the forehead. Reinforce by applying Eye Putti or eyelid glue to the bubbles.

10 Paint the bubbles with white acrylic paint. Apply in layers because the plastic will repel the paint. Mix red and blue acrylic paint.

11 Apply the red-purple paint, mixed in step 10, to the circumference of the bubbles.

12 Apply dark purple on the chin and smudge it using your fingertip.

13 Paint your model's face white using white grease paint excluding around the eyes. Do not apply evenly. Rather, make your application uneven.

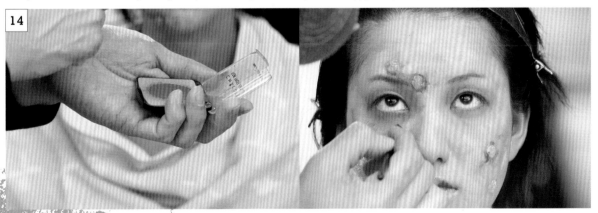

14 Overlay purple and red face paint around the eyes.

15

Mix black and brown face paint and apply along the lower eyelid.

16

Mix brown and blue grease paint and apply it to the base of the bubbles. Also, draw the blood vessels.

17

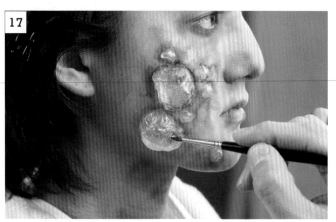

Add redness to the blisters.

18

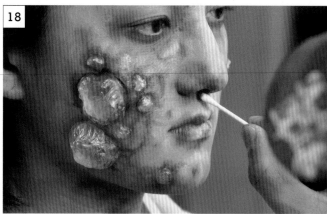

Paint the tip of the nose red to increase the appearance of a viral infection.

19

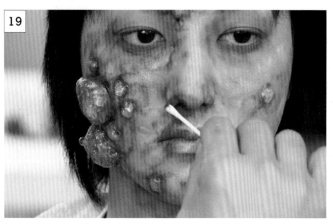

Add redness in a subtle manner. Add it to the base of the blisters and dents and then smudge using your finger.

20

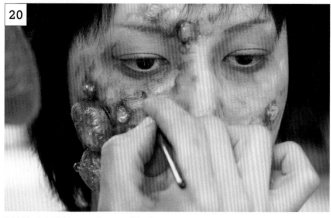

Add black to tighten up the overall look.

21

Mix skin color and blue and apply under the eyes as highlights.

COMPLETE!

Wet the hair to produce a greasy look to complete!

Burn Scar

by Akihito

This is a scar from a burn injury. Apply silicone putty to produce a burn scar and then paint with Skin Illustrator (alcohol-activated makeup paint).

[Materials]
3rd Degree (silicone modeling compound, light skin tone), TELESIS (adhesive for silicone), alcohol, skin illustrator (alcohol-activated makeup paint)

[Tools]
Plastic board, brushes, spatula

Model: Mick Ignis

01 Mix equal parts of 3rd Degree Part A and Part B. Apply the mixture to the plastic board and create a prosthetic for a burn scar. Just before the silicone hardens, smooth the surface with alcohol.

02 After the 3rd Degree has hardened, carefully remove it from the plastic board.

03 Bundle your model's hair neatly together. Hair and makeup is done by Mayumi Okamoto.

04 Use TELESIS to carefully attach the 3rd Degree prosthetic to your model's face.

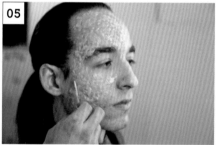

05 After the prosthetic is applied, add the 3rd Degree mixture directly on your model's face to conceal the edges of the prosthetic. Add to any areas where you think scars are lacking.

06 Apply color. Create depth using reddish brown, red, black, and orange.

07 On the other side of your model's face, apply The Phantom of the Opera-esque makeup and set the skin complexion.

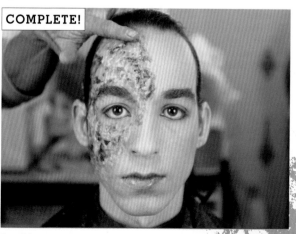

COMPLETE! Complete.

WOUND
makeup

MAKE UP FOR EVER
PROFESSIONAL – PARIS

PAINT MAKE UP AND SKIN CARE

by Akiko (MAKE UP FOR EVER)

MAKE UP FOR EVER makeup artist Akiko presents lectures on applying conceptual makeup and skin care, before and after general makeup application, that will help to enhance your final project. Special effects makeup is known for causing skin strain, so please be sure to read this section.

Akiko: Exclusive education manager and makeup artist at MAKE UP FOR EVER. After establishing her career as a professional makeup artist, she went to study in Paris. She studied hard and was named valedictorian of her class. Currently, she is actively involved in a wide range of projects for magazines, advertisements, and films. In addition, she teaches and gives makeup demonstrations. She is skilled at creative makeup for fashion and bodypainting. URL: www.makeupforever.jp

A professional makeup artist shares secrets for enhancing the final look of makeup

Skin Care 101: Before makeup application and after makeup is removed

01 **Before Makeup Application**

In cases where applying makeup on the skin produces noticeable indentations, applying a single white color evenly will actually make the indentations stand out. This will make the application appear very uneven. How do you deal with such conditions?

First, wash your model's face using a scrubbing face wash to eliminate excess sebum. When scrubbing face wash is not available, use a mix of oil and granulated sugar.

Apply alcohol-free skin toner until the skin becomes moist and wait for two to three minutes. Pinch the skin with your fingers to test for moisture. If the skin sticks to your fingers and if there is a certain plumpness, it is ready for makeup. If you apply moisturizer to the skin the special effects makeup adhesive won't adhere to the model's face, so be careful.

Apply concealer. The concealer used here can cover tattoos and contains medical grade anti-inflammatory properties. It is highly water-resistant and even entering a pool does not compromise the concealer's effectiveness. It can be applied in layers simply by pressing it down with powder. Conceal any skin unevenness by applying this concealer in layers until the unevenness becomes unnoticeable. The concealer can cover scars and bruises, but remember that the color will darken after a minute or so. Be sure to use a concealer that is one shade lighter than your model's skin. After setting with powder, water-activated makeup colors can be applied. In addition, glue for special effects makeup can be applied over the concealer.

02 **Removing Makeup**

When applying makeup daily, how thoroughly one removes that makeup will affect the next day's application. Don't forget that the skin is an important base. Always care for the skin in a careful and gentle manner.

To detach false eyelashes, start by detaching from the outer corner of the eye and move toward the inner corner, while pressing down on the outer corner of the eye. After detaching, clean the false eyelashes using eyelash glue remover.

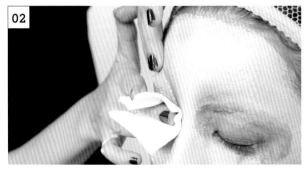

The areas around the eyes and mouth can be quite delicate, so be sure to use specialized makeup remover or cleansing oil makeup remover. Don't rub hard! Remove dark colored makeup using cleansing oil makeup remover.

Lightly wipe off the lip area with specialized makeup remover or cleansing oil makeup remover.

04 Put some makeup remover on a cotton pad and then wipe off the makeup, beginning from the center of the face and moving outward. Careful! Do not wipe downward as doing so will cause the facial muscles to sag.

05 Water-activated paint can be removed by washing with body soap. Using a soft dish sponge works best.

06 Put some cleansing oil on your hand and work it in multiple times to remove stubborn pigments. Over the cleansing oil, apply skin toner in a circular motion with your fingers to emulsify the oil. Then, wipe off to remove the pigment. This is a sure fire method to help remove difficult makeup.

07 Use cotton swabs to remove detailed areas, such as the edges of the eyes, where makeup still remains.

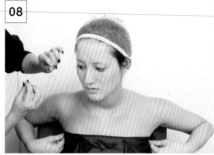

08 Wash the face using lukewarm water.

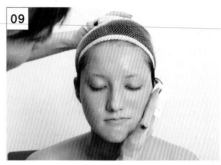

09 Take plenty of skin toner on a cotton pad and then wipe the face from the center outward.

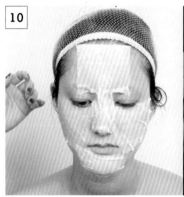

10 Divide a cotton pad that has been saturated with skin toner into five sheets. Put one sheet on the forehead, both cheeks, chin, and nose to moisturize.

11 Leave cotton sheets on the face for five to ten minutes at most. If the sheets are left on the face too long, the cotton starts to remove moisture from the skin. This treatment should be kept short.

12 Apply face serum to condition the skin. Choose face serum that contains hyaluronic acid and seaweed extract to help maintain healthy skin.

COMPLETE! At the end, you should apply lotion so that the skin toner and face serum doesn't evaporate. Complete!

Applying makeup using water-activated colors

Conceptual Makeup

This section introduces techniques and designs for an even application and beautiful finish when employing water-activated colors. Oil-activated colors can be laid over water-activated colors. However, oil-activated colors will not stay when laid over water-activated colors. Make sure you don't get the steps in the wrong order.

Model: Aya

Design sketch. The theme for this makeup is "technicolor." White is the base color and brown-beige was added in gradations. Limit the use of white to attenuate the traditional Japanese-style look. The hairstyle is a 1960's inspired mushroom cut.

01 | Base Makeup

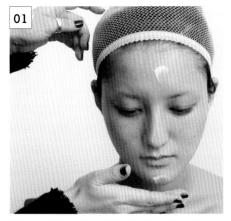

01 After preparing your model's skin, by applying skin toner, etc., apply primer to condition.

02 Apply concealer until your model's skin becomes smooth.

03 Set the concealer with loose face powder. The base process helps to prevent pigmentation.

04 Dissolve the water-activated colors with water until they become cream-like. Mix beige and white.

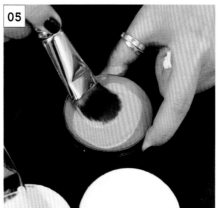

05 Similarly, dissolve brown until it has a cream-like consistency. Use a firm nylon-bristled brush with uniform bristles.

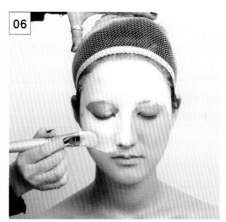

06 Apply the color to the intended area all at once. Adjust brush strokes by lightly brushing the area while applying very little pressure.

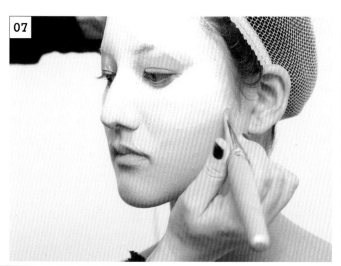

07

Apply brown to the lower-half of the face.

08

Blend the borders where the two colors meet in a similar manner to blending colors when you paint.

09

Extend the brown to just under the chin. Intently brush, using uniform pressure, and apply thoroughly .

10

Apply beige, thinned with water, to the eyelid and the crease of the eye using a small-bristled brush. Let the beige dry and then apply beige to the edges of the eye. Water-activated colors will dry without powdering.

11

Pour some shimmering powder (white gold) on a piece of tissue paper. Then, put it evenly on the bristles of a brush. Apply on the face to alter the overall texture.

12

Apply some shimmering powder (golden orange) on the lower-half of the face.

01

Apply grease paint. Soften the outline using a clean brush. Grease paint has more vivid color development than water-activated colors.

02

Lightly apply eyeshadow over the grease paint. Just lay it over the grease paint because any rubbing motion will cause the grease paint to come off.

03

Apply yellow grease paint. Then, overlay yellow eyeshadow.

04

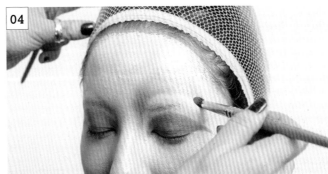

Apply shimmering powder (neon fuscia) to the pink area.

05

Add shadows. Use red-purple on the pink area. Use green and black on the green area.

06

Add gradations under the eyes using mixed black and green.

07

Curl the eyelashes using a curler and then apply mascara. Apply black water-proofed eyeliner along the upper and lower lash line.

08

Attach feathers to the false eyelashes first. Then attach the false eyelashes, with white beads attached, while slightly offsetting them from the feather attached false eyelashes.

01

Mix waterproof liquid converter and pink colored "blacklight" pigment until it becomes thick.

02

Apply the mixture beginning with the center of the lips. The mixture is water-soluble, so it will dry without applying powder.

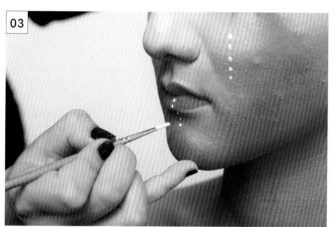

03

Use water-activated color to draw white dots.

04

Add a pair of color contact lenses.

COMPLETE!

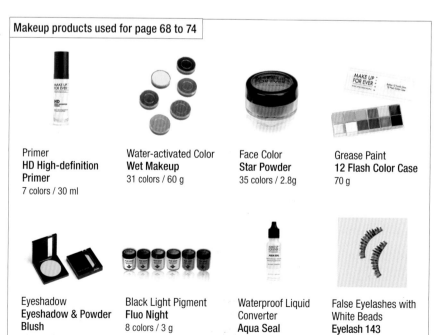

Makeup products used for page 68 to 74

Primer
HD High-definition Primer
7 colors / 30 ml

Water-activated Color
Wet Makeup
31 colors / 60 g

Face Color
Star Powder
35 colors / 2.8g

Grease Paint
12 Flash Color Case
70 g

Eyeshadow
Eyeshadow & Powder Blush
96 colors / 2.5 g

Black Light Pigment
Fluo Night
8 colors / 3 g

Waterproof Liquid Converter
Aqua Seal
12 ml

False Eyelashes with White Beads
Eyelash 143

Throw on a wig to complete.

CHAPTER 02

MASKS

A COLLECTION OF BLOODTHIRSTY SERIAL KILLERS AND HORROR MASKS

A *Phantom of the Opera*-esque mask that is formed by embossing a heated plastic sheet over a face cast

Eyewitness

by AKIHITO

Photographer : Akihito, Assistant : Mayumi Okamoto, Making photo : Hiroshi Furusho, Model : Mick Ignis

[Materials]
Lifecast (your model's face cast, any face cast that you can use, or a drawing cast), plastic sheet, polyester putty, aluminum wire, adhesive, primer (white), epoxy putty, spray paint (gold), alcohol-activated paint (i.e. brown and black from Skin Illustrator), oil paint

[Tools]
Scissors, utility blade, heat gun, marker, airbrush, sponge

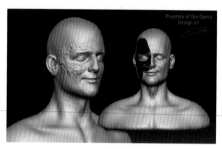
Design Sketch

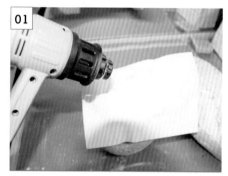
01
Place a plastic sheet over the face cast. Heat it using a heat gun.

02
When the plastic sheet becomes soft enough to manipulate, press it against the face cast and massage to form.

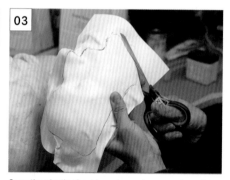
03
Once the plastic sheet is embossed, remove from the face cast and trim off the excess.

04
Glue aluminum wire on the mask as an embellishment.

05
Apply polyester putty in a dabbing motion with a sponge to produce texture. Apply white primer as your base color.

06
Spray gold paint over the base color. Airbrush brown and black alcohol-activated paint to color the mask.

07
Add black and brown oil paints to produce a weathered look to complete.

A mask made out of *washi* and polymer clay

J Mask

by Tomo Hyakutake

Photographer : Hironobu Onodera, Model : Maya

[Materials]
Lifecast (your model's face cast, any face cast that you can use, or a drawing cast), oil-based clay, woodworking glue, Japanese calligraphy paper, water-activated paint (black), Hearty Soft White, acrylic paint (white, moss-green, red, blue), false nails, stage blood

[Tools]
Brushes, pail, spatula, paper cup

Hearty Soft White is an air-dry modeling clay that is known for making fake sweets, but it is surprisingly suitable for making masks. This is a novel material. It is a lightweight modeling clay with a super fine texture that allows for painting without melting.

Sculpt the face of the mask using oil-based clay (if a face cast is not available, sculpt without using a cast at all).

Pour woodworking glue into a paper cup and apply on the oil-based clay face using a brush.

Pour some water into a pail and add woodworking glue. Mix them to dissolve. Dip Japanese calligraphy paper in the pail to soak and then apply this paper-maché to the face sculpture.

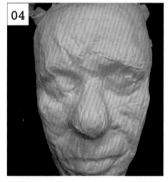

While the papier-maché is still slightly wet, remove it from the face sculpture. Then, leave the papier-maché to dry completely for a few days.

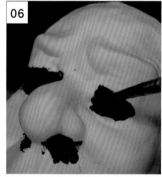

Fill in both eyes and nostrils with black water-based paint.

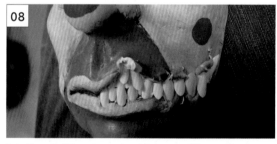

Cut off a part of the polymer clay at the corner of the mouth using a sturdy spatula, then glue false nails on the mask to make teeth (see photo above).

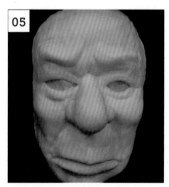

Use Hearty Soft White (lightweight modeling polymer clay) to sculpt onto the papier-maché to further add details.

Mix white and moss-green acrylic paint in a 9 to 1 ratio. After the black paint has dried, apply the mixed color to the entirety of the mask. Apply thinly so the color underneath the paint is still visible. Paint the nose, eyebrows, and other facial features using red and blue.

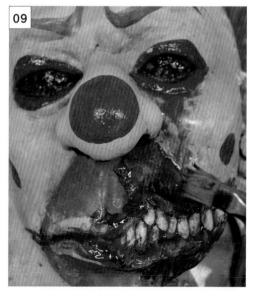

Apply some stage blood to complete.

Paper towels and tissue paper produce rough skin texture – this mask resembles Michael from the slasher film *Halloween*

Michael Yoshi

by Kakusei Fujiwara

Photographer : Hironobu Onodera, Model : Kakusei

[Materials]
Face Cast (you can use a commercially available mask), liquid latex, paper towel, spray adhesive, rigid polyurethane foam sheet, Bond G (multi-purpose adhesive), woodworking glue, tissue paper, acrylic spray paint, a piece of sheer stage curtain fabric (or powernet mesh fabric), wig, sawdust mixed liquid latex, oil-based stain (walnut)

[Tools]
Scissors, hake brush, airbrush

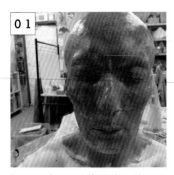
01 Prepare a face cast (if you do not have a face cast, use a commercially available mask instead), and coat the face cast with liquid latex.

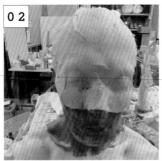
02 Prepare paper towels and then paste them over the face cast before the latex dries.

03 Spray adhesive over the paper towels and lay down another layer.

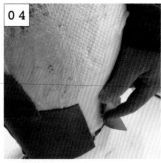
04 Cover the face cast with four to five layers of paper towel. Glue a piece of rigid polyurethane foam sheeting around the neck using Bond G. This will prevent the mask from becoming distorted.

05 Dilute woodworking glue with some water and glue on tissue paper over the paper towel to form a mask.

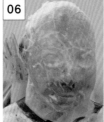
06 Once the form of the mask has reached your intended shape, give it a coat of woodworking glue.

07 Spray on acrylic paint.

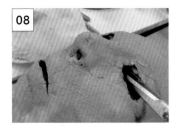
08 Use scissors to trim off areas of the mask for both eye sockets, nostrils, and the mouth.

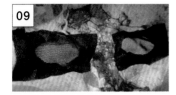
09 Prepare either a piece of sheer stage curtain fabric or powernet mesh fabric and glue it on inside the mask to cover the opening for the eyes (this will conceal the eyes of the performer wearing the mask).

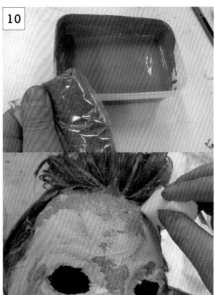
10 Glue on a wig using Bond G. Dab sawdust mixed in liquid latex along the hairline to conceal where the wig is glued. Then add some weathering.

Airbrush oil-based stain (walnut) on the shaded areas of the mask. Add necessary effects at the filming/shooting site, but for now it's complete.

Using Sunpelca® Foamed Polyethylene Sheet, *That* Mask is Here!

From Crystal Lake

by Akiteru Nakada

Photographer : Hironobu Onodera, Model : Akiteru

[Materials]
Fando (stone powder clay), Sunpelca® (foam polyethylene sheet), rivets, liquitex (white, brown, black), vinyl tape (red), paper for a pattern, spray adhesive, metal snaps, spray paint, elastic cord

[Tools]
Burner, scissors, leathercraft hole punch, rivet setting tool, work gloves

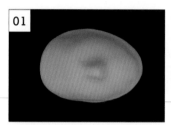

Sculpt the ice hockey mask shape using Fando (stone powder clay) to make a mold.

Heat Sunpelca® (foam polyethylene sheet) using a burner to soften the sheet. Be careful not to overheat it or it may catch fire. Be sure to wear gloves.

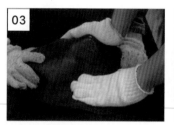

Press the heated Sunpelca® sheet against the mold.

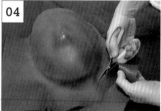

Trim off the excess foam polyethylene sheet.

Decide on the positions where you intend to punch holes in the mask. Then punch 8 to 10 mm (1/4" to 3/8") diameter holes using a leathercraft hole punch.

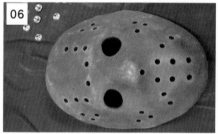

The above photo shows where holes were punched. At the left corner of the photo, it shows some rivets that are going to be attached to the mask.

Apply white Liquitex on the mask as a base.

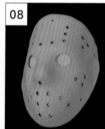

The photo above shows where white Liquitex has been applied.

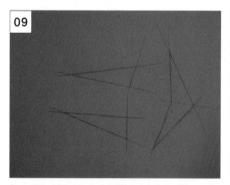

On a piece of paper, sketch the red designs. Then, cut each component off to create a pattern.

Use a spray adhesive to glue the pattern on a piece of red vinyl tape. Trim off the tape according to the pattern. Tape it on the mask and then peel off the pattern.

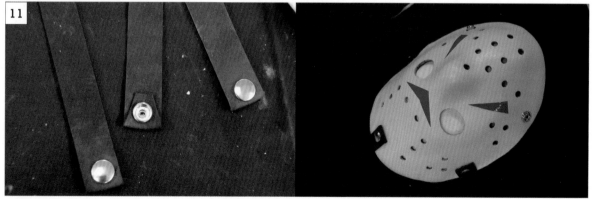

Attach studs for the metal snaps on a piece of elastic and then attach the sockets on the mask. Fasten the metal snap to attach the elastic to the mask. Add some weathering using Liquitex and spray paint to complete.

The "Iron Sukekiyo" mask is made combining commercially available components like a plastic mask and samurai-hair wig

IRON•SUKEKIYO

by Yoshinori Dohi

Photographer : Hironobu Onodera, Model : Yuriko

Design Sketch
Shizuma Aoyama severely injured his face on a battlefield and became a prisoner of war. Together with Sukekiyo Inugami, Shizuma secretly developed an armor for escaping from a POW camp. They named the armor "Iron Sukekiyo" and started it up.
The theme for this mask is to create something combining different components together without modeling.

[Materials]
Plastic mask, samurai-hair wig, frying pan and bowl (from a dollar store), ladle, tape, aluminum wire mesh, round tin can lid (130 mm/5" diameter), bottle cap, pull tabs, rivets, rubber tubing, lead wire and other detailing materials, binding wire, zip ties, screws, black fabric, sheer stage curtain fabric, gray-color primer, metallic red color primer, clear yellow spray paint, gunmetal or various silver-color paints, oil-based stain, thinner, masking tape, super glue, epoxy adhesive, Bond G (multi-purpose adhesive), marker, midget light bulb, elastic cord

[Tools]
Electric drills, drill bits, sandpaper, utility blade, scissors, pliers, wire snips

01

Temporarily put the mask and a frying pan together. When you are satisfied with how they are put together, mark the positions where they will join. Drill holes at the marked positions. For aluminum, use a metalworking drill bit. For stainless steel, be sure to use a drill bit specifically made for stainless steel. Secure the components together using binding wire and zip ties.

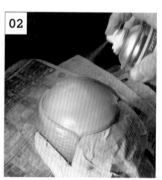

02

Mask the head area, then spay on primer.

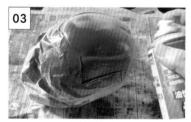

03

After the primer has dried, spray on some metallic red. Be sure to use adequate ventilation while spraying.

04

After the metallic red paint has dried, mask the head area again. Spray clear yellow on the metal parts to create a gold color.

05

Split the casing of the tape you purchased at a dollar store. Then, glue on a piece of aluminum wire mesh (see photo).

06

Use epoxy adhesive to attach it to the mask.

07

To cover the ends of the binding wire inside the mask, bend the ends and glue a piece of black fabric over them. This will protect the face of whoever wears the mask.

08

At the back side of the mask, attach a tin can lid to make a base. Add more details by attaching bottle caps, detached pot handles, and metal mesh to the base. Use a pipe clamp to attach the tin can to the mask. Join the components with rubber tubing while carefully considering the movements of the mask wearer.

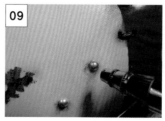

09

Add details with rivets, rubber tubing, etc., as desired.

10

Add silver or a gunmetal color on the top of the head using a brush. Apply oil-based stain using a brush or an airbrush to create a weathered look. Roughly sand the metal parts using sandpaper. Glue a piece of mesh fabric inside the mask on the eyes to complete.

(Extra)
Drill a hole in a bowl and attach a small light bulb for
the glove. Attach pull tabs on the bowl using binding
wire and put an elastic cord around each tab.

A mask made by combining items purchased at a dollar store, using as few specialty materials and tools as possible

SCREAM!...

Behind the mask there was a similar looking face!

by Yoshinori Dohi

Photographer : Hironobu Onodera, Model : Yuriko

Design Sketch

[Materials]
Two types of Ghost Face mask (ones that you can find at a dollar store), paper towel, woodworking glue, false nails, imitation cherry prop, wig that you don't need, watercolor (white, red, cream, blue, brown, black, etc.), lacquer spray (black, clear yellow, clear orange, smokey gray, clear, etc.)

[Tools]
Paint brushes, popsicle sticks

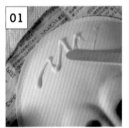

01 Prepare two types of Ghost Face mask. One is good quality and the other is not so good. Apply woodworking glue on the mask that is not as good.

02 Glue paper towel on the mask using woodworking glue.

03 Glue the paper towel so as to make use of its texture for details.

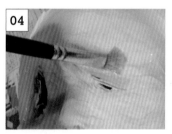

04 Cover the mask with paper towel and leave to dry. Coat the mask with woodworking glue diluted with water and then allow to dry.

05 Paint the mask using watercolors to create an eerie look.

06 Once the paint has dried, spray on some clear yellow, clear orange, and smoky gray lacquer paint to adjust the look of the mask.

07 Paint an eyeball on the imitation cherry prop. If you can't find a cherry prop, use anything that has a spherical shape that resembles an eyeball.

08 Mix red watercolor paint with woodworking glue. Then, apply on a flat surface while making streaks. Once dried, peel from the flat surface. Use paste where the mask and the eyeball meet to look like the veins.

09 Attach nail tips to the inside of the mouth for teeth.

10 Glue on some wig hair using woodworking glue.

11 Apply woodworking glue or lacquer spray to make the surface of the mask more lustrous.

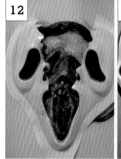

12 Split the good quality mask and attach the other mask inside using adhesive.

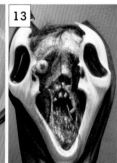

13 Attach the black hood to the back to complete

Toy Telephone, vinyl leather, modular cable, etc. Combine these components to create this crazy looking mask

Hello, Readers.

by Soichi Umezawa

Photographer : Hironobu Onodera, Model : Shigeru Okuse

[Materials]
Toy telephone, wire mesh, rigid urethane (or styrene foam), water-based putty, primer, vinyl leather, wire, super glue, clear plastic dome, telephone parts, telephone cord, zip tie, cable protector, Bond G (multi-purpose adhesive), Liquitex

[Tools]
Utility blade, scissors, pliers, wire snips, brushes, sandpaper

Design Sketch

01

Prepare the handset of a toy telephone. If one is not available, carve rigid urethane to make the shape of a handset.

02

Once the handset is ready, spray on some primer. Coat using water-based putty to conceal the rough texture of the rigid urethane. Sand with sandpaper and then add primer. Repeat this process until the surfaces of the handset become smooth.

03

Bend the wire mesh in the shape of a face. Cut out the mouth area.

04

Paint the unused handset phone holder white. Attach that to the wire mesh using wires.

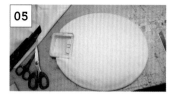

05

Glue vinyl leather on the wire mesh using Bond G.

06

Use Liquitex to paint an eyeball on the inside of each clear plastic dome.

07

Carve a piece of rigid urethane in the shape of a nose. Then, glue modular cable on the nose-shape.

08

Cut out the nose portion of the vinyl leather that was glued on the wire mesh. Attach the modular cable covered urethane nose.

09

Glue the eyeballs on using super glue. Loop some zip ties around the eyes.

10

Secure some cable protector to the wire mesh using wire. This makes the hair of the mask.

Attach a dial on each cheek. Attach telephone cords around the face of the mask.

088

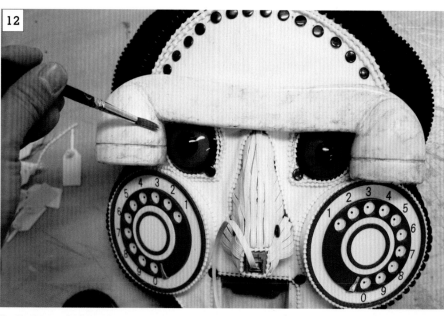

12

Use Liquitex to paint the mask and add a weathered look.

This papier-mâché mask has an adorable scariness that is similar to *The Nightmare Before Christmas*

Trick or Treat

by Makiko Kono

Photographer : Yosuke Komatsu, Model : Makiko

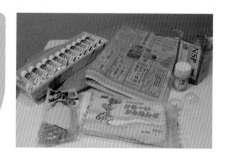

[Materials]
Cardboard, duct tape, oil-based clay, newspaper, water, woodworking glue, lightweight paper clay, acrylic paint, Kofun Gesso (water-soluble acrylic paint surface preparation medium mixed with ground shells), silk flower

[Tools]
Scissors, sandpaper, paper towel, carving tools, hake brush, brushes, paper cup, blow dryer

---

01

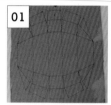

In order to allow the mold to be easily removed later, draw a diagram on a piece of cardboard - as shown in the photo above - according to the size of the mask. This will make a foundation where the mold will be sculpted (if you have a face cast, you can use that instead). Draw the diagram after roughly measuring the size of the face. For example, put your face against a piece of copying paper, etc.

02

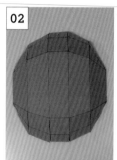

Cut the cardboard along the diagram. Build the foundation and secure the joined seams using duct tape.

03

Sculpt the overall shape of the mask using oil-based clay on the foundation.

04

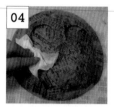

Tear some newspaper into small pieces and soak them in water. Then, lay down the pieces of wet newspaper as to cover the clay mold. Cut a piece of newspaper into a long and narrow strip using scissors. This will cover the outer edge of the mask and produce a clean finish. At this point, apply pressure to the paper towel to remove excess moisture in the newspaper pieces.

05

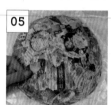

For easy application, dilute woodworking glue with a small amount of water. Then, apply the diluted glue over the newspaper. Be careful not to dilute the glue too much as that will compromise its adhesion strength. Lay down another layer of torn newspaper pieces while the glue is still wet.

06

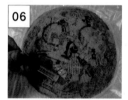

After layering the newspaper pieces, apply woodworking glue using a brush by pressing the bristles against the newspaper to remove any trapped air. Repeat this process about seven times.

07

Blow dry the surface. After it has dried, remove the clay foundation. Blow dry the mask again from the backside. After the layers of newspaper have dried completely, apply woodworking glue to the inside of the mask. Allow to dry.

08

Tear lightweight paper clay into small pieces and then dissolve them in water. Add some woodworking glue and mix. Apply the mixture to the mask. Allow to dry.

09

Use lightweight paper clay to sculpt detailed designs on the mask. After the clay has dried, smooth the surface with sandpaper.

10

Dissolve some lightweight paper clay with water and woodworking glue. Apply the mixture to anchor the paper clay on the mask.

11

After the mixture has dried, apply Kofun Gesso on the mask to bring out a matte finish.

12

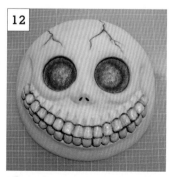

Paint using acrylic paint. To produce a realistic look, apply woodworking glue exclusively on the teeth. This will make them look shiny. Attach a silk flower on one eye to complete.

A crown style mask with a stiff frame made from FRP

Akagami

by Tomonobu Iwakura

Photographer : Hironobu Onodera, Model : Sachi Yanagida

[Materials]
Face cast, NSP clay, spray lacquer (clear), mold making silicone (KE-12), catalyst (curing agent), FRP, talc powder, fiberglass mat (cut into pieces), water-based Clay, fiberglass, primer, hobby color (black), gauze

[Tools]
Utility blade, brush, hake brush, carving tools

Design Sketch

01 Use NSP clay to sculpt a model of the mask on the face cast. Sculpting the model out of clay requires a face cast so it is convenient to have one. Please refer to p.86, *Conceptual Special Effects Makeup 2*, for making face casts. Spray clear lacquer on the sculpture to help the mold release.

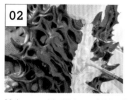

02 Make a mold of this sculpture. At first, mix mold making silicone (KE-12) with curing agent in a 100 to 2 ~ 3 ratio. Apply this mixture on the sculpture using a brush.

03 After the first application has cured, apply a second layer. Then lay down some gauze to cover the sculpture.

04 After the second layer has dried, apply the third layer, the hard shell, and leave to cure.

05 Fill the undercuts (dented areas) using clay.

Use water-based clay to build a wall along the centerline that runs vertically over the nose line. Spay lacquer (clear) as a mold release.

07 In order to reinforce the silicone, apply a layer of GEL poly, a mixture of FRP, talc powder, and small pieces of fiberglass mat.

Apply fiberglass.

Apply FRP to saturate the fiberglass.

10 Once the FRP has solidified, remove the silicone from the face cast. Then, remove the wall built with the water-based clay. Apply Vaseline as a mold release. Remove any clay still attached on the silicone once the mold is ready.

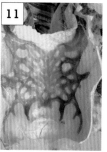

11 Apply a layer of GEL poly inside the mold.

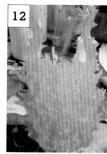

12 Lay down fiberglass over the GEL poly and leave about twenty minutes to cure. Remove any burrs.

13 Color the mask. Apply primer before painting.

14 Paint the mask using Hobby Color to complete.

CHAPTER 03

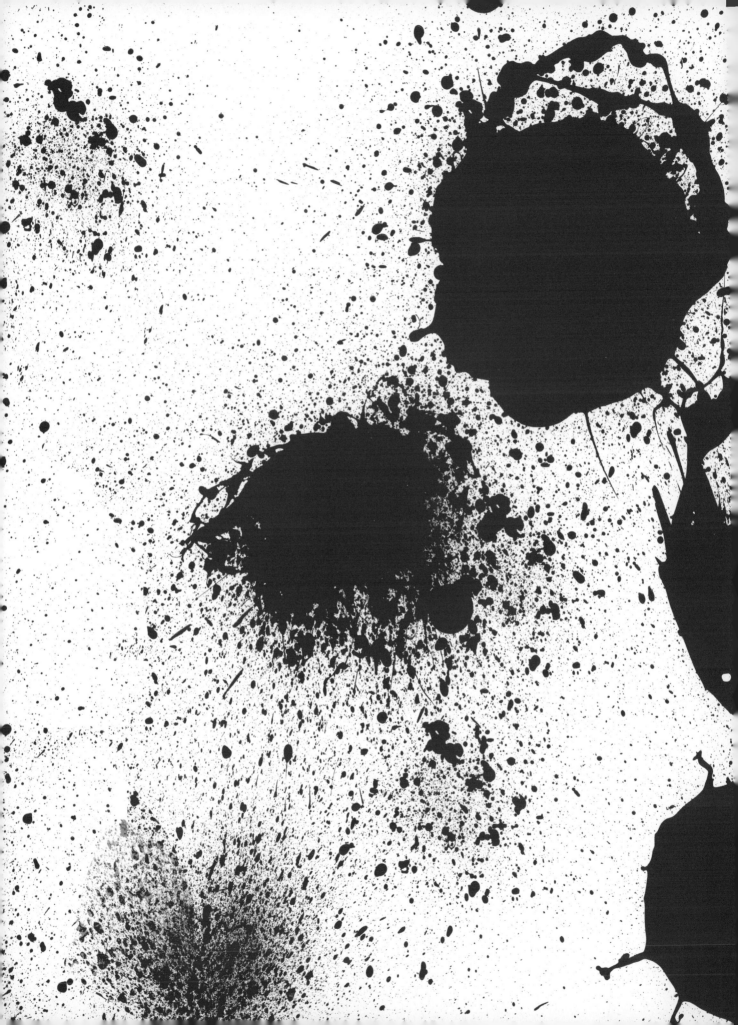

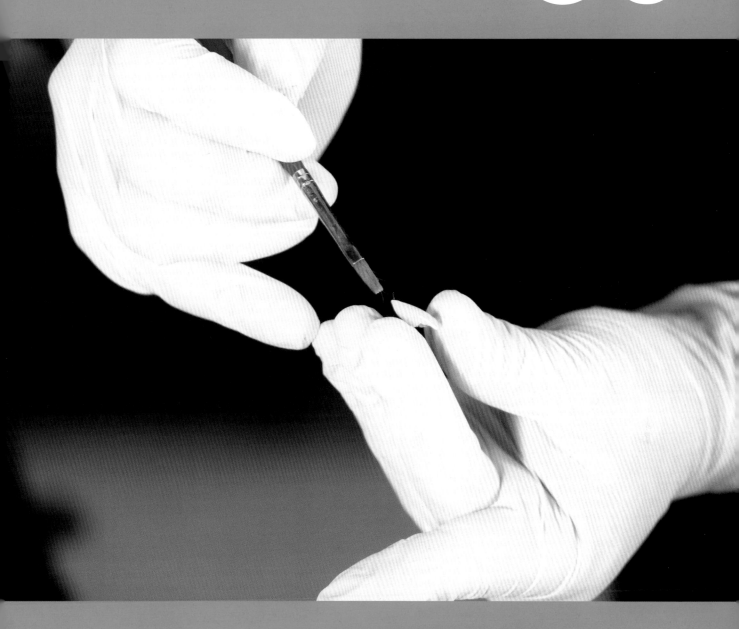

MODELING AND BANDAGES

How to Make Fake Fangs

by Tomonobu Iwakura

Using commercially available false nails, these fangs are easy to make. The point is to match the nail color with your teeth.

[Materials]
False nails (dollar store), NSP clay, dental acrylic, curing agent, ethanol, denture adhesive (i.e. Polygrip), Skin Illustrator

[Tools]
Sandpaper, nose hair scissors, carving tools, dropper, dremel, blow dryer, cotton swabs, scissors, tissue paper, cosmetic spatula, brush

01

Prepare two of the same size false nails. Choose nails that match your teeth. Use nose hair scissors to trim the nails into the desired fang shape.

02

Sand off nails to round trimmed edges.

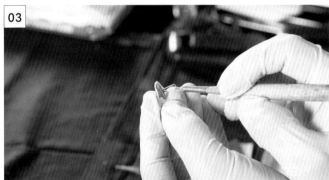

03

On the backside of the nail, sculpt the shape of the fang using NSP clay.

04

Put some dental acrylic powder on a flat surface.

05

Use a dropper to place some curing agent on the dental acrylic powder. Then mix.

06

Apply the dental acrylic mixture thinly over the NSP clay sculpted on the nail.

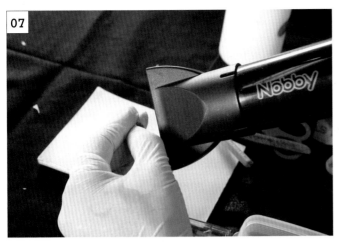

07

Blow dry to cure the dental acrylic.

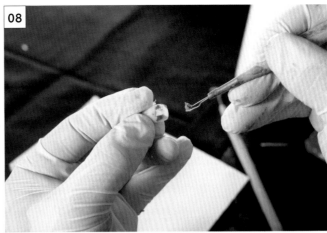

08

Once cured, pick out the NSP clay.

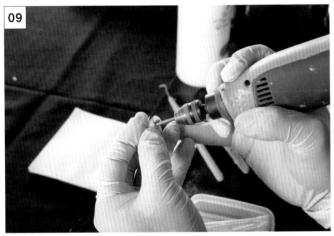

09

Use a Dremel to shave out the inside to make some space.

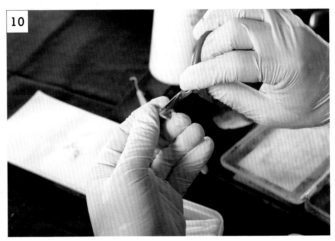

10

Make the fang opening using scissors.

11

Sand off the opening and hollow the inside of the fang to create a space where the real tooth will go.

12

Pour ethanol inside the fang and clean using a cotton swab.

13

Place the fang close to a real tooth to compare color.

14

Paint the fang with Skin Illustrator thinned using ethanol.

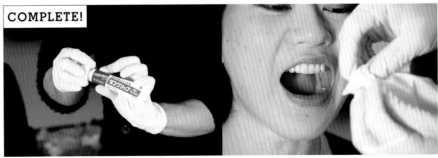

COMPLETE!

Take some denture adhesive on a cosmetic spatula and apply it inside the fang. Wipe moisture from the tooth where the fang goes and apply denture adhesive. Firmly press the fang against the tooth. Once the fang is secured, it's complete.

How to Make Nail-Pierced Skin

by Tomonobu Iwakura

Pierce round tipped 6" nails through fake skin made from silicone. It should look like a gory wound.

[Materials]
A plaster working foundation, NSP clay, plaster, burlap, Baldiez, acetone, Gel 10 - part A, part B, deadener

[Tools]
Airbrush, clamps, Skin Illustrator, 6" nails, hake brush

01

Thinly paste NSP clay over a foundation (flat surface) made from plaster. Make it a little thinner towards the edges.

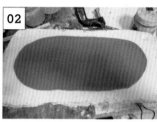

02

The skin model is complete.

03

To build the flesh, encase the sculpture using any excess clay.

04

Dissolve plaster with water and then coat the clay using a hake brush.

05

Apply another layer of plaster and then wrap with burlap to reinforce.

06

Now the mold is complete. Remove the clay inside the flesh. Apply Vaseline as a mold release.

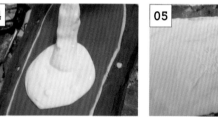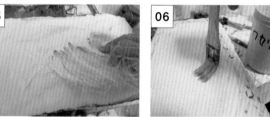

07

Dilute one part Baldiez with ten parts acetone. Apply four layers of the diluted Baldiez using an airbrush.

08

Mix Gel 10 part A, part B, and deadener in a 1:1:3 ratio. Mix well and then pour in the mold.

09

Put the plaster foundation on the mold and press firmly using clamps.

10

Peel the prosthetic off the mold.

11

Push 6" nails through the prosthetic.

COMPLETE!

Paint the prosthetic using Skin Illustrator to complete.

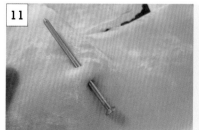

How to Make a Long Leather Bracelet With Attached Nails

by Tomonobu Iwakura

Attach dollar store golf tees to a piece of synthetic leather to produce this bracelet.

[Materials]
Synthetic leather, super glue, golf tees (dollar store tees will suffice)

[Tools]
Scissors, airbrush

01 Cut synthetic leather using scissors.

02 Make sure the leather strips are uniform in width.

03 Glue the strips together while making cross joints.

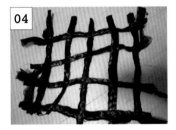

04 One piece is complete. Make sure this piece is wide enough to wrap around your arm.

05 Prepare golf tees.

06 Apply super glue at the joints and glue on a tee.

07 The photo above shows when all the tees have been applied.

08 Airbrush each tee black.

COMPLETE! Produce an overall weathered look to complete!

How Put on a Bandage

by Tomonobu Iwakura

This is the proper way to put on a bandage that won't come undone, as taught by a nurse. Remember, always wrap bandages from the lower to the upper position.

[Materials]
Two rolls of bandage, gauze, surgical tape

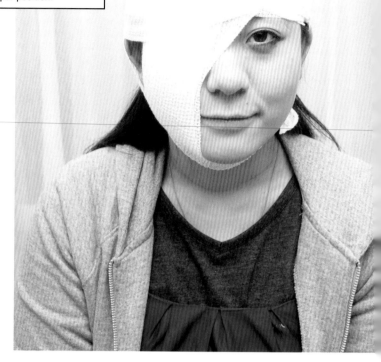

Model: Kanako Kitaochi

[1] Bandage on a Face

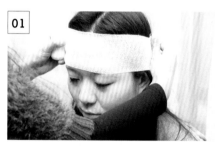

01 Align the bottom edge of the bandage above the eyebrow of your model.

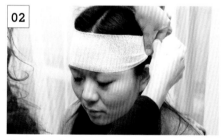

02 Wrap the bandage clockwise around the head one time. Put the bandage *over* the ears so the bandage stays in place.

03 After wrapping twice around the head, position the bandage on the injured eye.

TIP
This side is the right side. The side that touches the patient's skin is the reverse side.

04 Place a piece of gauze, with ointment on it, on the injured eye.

05 Slide the bandage down to cover the eye in such a manner that the bandage holds the gauze in place.

06

Temporarily hold the bandage on the jaw.

07

Pass the bandage under the chin while holding it taut. Wrap gently though because if the bandage is too tight it may be uncomfortable.

08

Pass the bandage behind the ear on the opposite side of the injured eye, then go up to the head.

09

Once again, wrap from the bandaged side of the head to under the chin.

10

Fold down the end of the bandage and secure using surgical tape.

11

The first roll of the bandage ends here. Fold the end and secure using surgical tape.

12

Once again, wrap the head. Place another bandage roll on the forehead.

13

Wrap the bandage once around the forehead without covering the ears.

14

Bring the bandage down over the eye.

15

Pass under the chin.

16

Bring the bandage up, passing behind the ear, then up to the head.

17

Wrap once around the forehead.

COMPLETE!

Secure the end using surgical tape to complete.

In the case of a real head injury, protect the wound using thicker bandages and a tubular net bandage.

[2] Arm Bandage

01 Place a bandage on the wrist of your model.

02 Wrap clockwise around the wrist one time.

03 Wrap again.

04 After wrapping twice, bring the bandage up at an angle.

05 Push the bandage down with your pinky and bring down to form a twist. Doing so helps the bandage stay in place.

06 Wrap around once.

07 As you wrap the arm, gradually move toward upper arm.

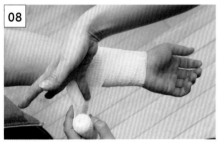

08 Again, push down the bandage with your pinky to twist the bandage.

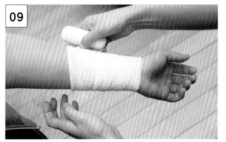

09 Continue to wrap upward.

10 When finished, fold the end down.

11 Secure with surgical tape.

COMPLETE!

Complete!

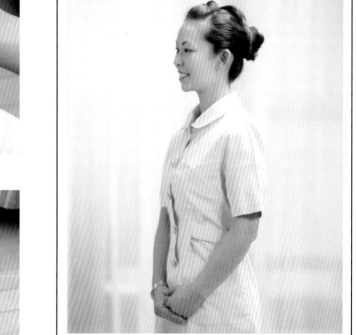

Profile

Chiharu Onodera
Chiharu is an experienced nurse. She works in an orthopedic ward.

STEP-BY-STEP

Step-by-Step Instructions

Lace Piercing

SFX MAKEUP 01

by Akihito

Corset piercings can be seen in overseas fashion magazines. Many people find corset piercings attractive simply as beautiful alterations of the human body. Some corset piercings are sold as personal adornments. However, here special effects makeup is used to render aesthetics that are similar to commercially available piercings without actual piercing.

[Materials]
Rings, lace, naphtha (lighter fluid for a dollar store lighter), alcohol, NSP clay (medium hardness, brown), silicone for making a mold, Pros-Aide, plastic sheet for tattooing, body paint

[Tools]
Clay carving tools, compressor, tattoo sheet, airbrush, freezer

Model: Mick Ignis

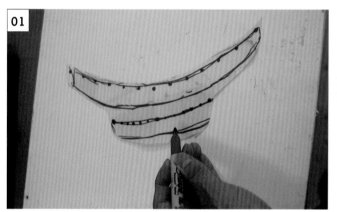

01 Decide on the position of the piercing.

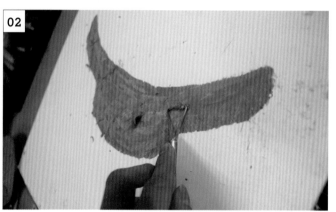

02 Begin to sculpt an appliance using clay, while confirming the piercing's position. Then go ahead and finish sculpting.

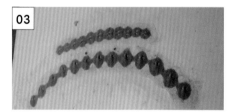

03 The photo above shows when the clay sculpture is complete.

04 Build walls around the sculpture and cast using silicone.

05 After pouring silicone, remove air bubbles using compressed air.
Assistant: Mayumi Okamoto

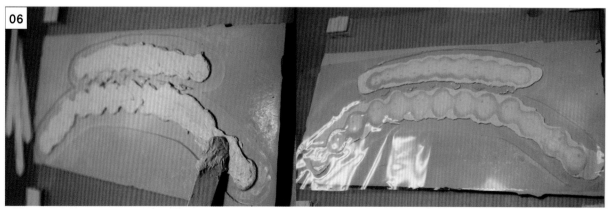

06 After the silicone has set, apply Pros-Aide to the mold. Lay a plastic sheet over the Pros-Aide. Since silicone is a soft material, before pouring be sure to put down a thin piece of wood. That way you can carry the mold wherever you wish. Put the mold, as is, in the freezer and leave for a couple of hours. The Pros-Aide will start to thaw right after the mold is taken out of the freezer, so remove any burrs immediately after the appliance is released from the mold.

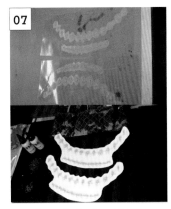

07

Leave the synthetic skin made from Pros-Aide to dry. In the meantime, prepare for makeup.

08

Mark holes on the backside of the tattoo sheet in order to make sure the piercings are symmetrical.

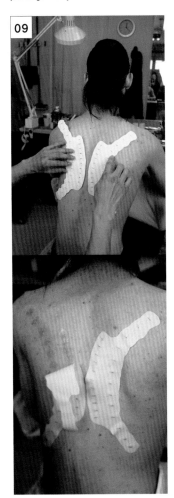

09

Begin to apply makeup. Carefully apply the synthetic skin to your model's back.

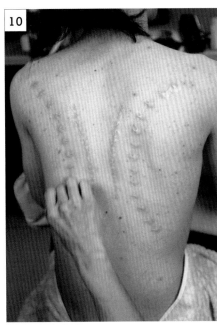

10

Smooth off the edges of the synthetic skin using alcohol.

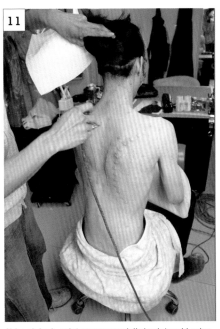

11

Airbrush body paint on your model's back to add color.

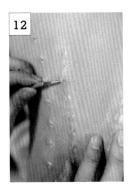

12

Again, pierce holes in the synthetic skin to make adding the rings easier.

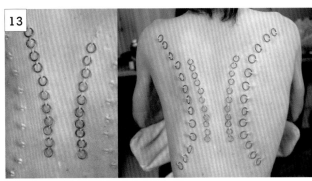

13

Put a ring in each pierced hole.

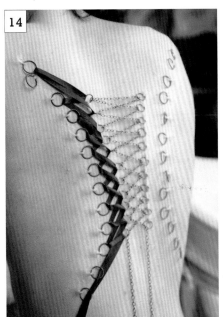

14

Carefully lace up the pierced rings.

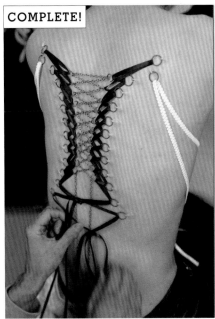

COMPLETE!

Complete!

Chase Down

Model: Kohei Sato, a rugby player

by Akihito

The concept here is that these wounds were caused by torture. Once caught, this person was beaten. Initially, their lip was split but then they escaped. However, they were caught and beaten again. In the end the captive's nose was broken, the eye was swollen, and they began to throw up blood.
The photos introduced in the gallery section have a progressive story-line.

[Materials]
Gelatin appliance (upper and lower lip, corner of the mouth, nose, eyes, cheeks), water, skin toner, Pros-Aide, powder, acrylic paint (two types of red, dark brown, purple, black, ocher), Liquitex blood (Liquitex Quinacridone red-orange + gel + medium), stage blood

[Tools]
Brush, cotton swabs, paper cups

01	Split Lip

01 Apply a gelatin appliance to the corner of the mouth using Pros-Aide.

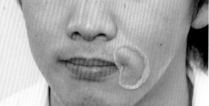

02 Apply another gelatin appliance on the upper and lower lip.

03 Use skin toner to dissolve away the edges of the appliance. This will remove flashing.

04 Put acrylic paint (two types of red, burnt brown, purple, black, ocher) on a palette. Add redness on the cheekbone to produce the hemorrhaging caused by punching.

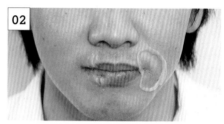

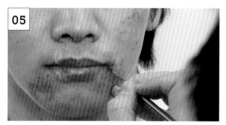

05 Add redness to the appliance on the corner of the mouth.

06 Add redness to the splits on the lips and add shadows using brown. Apply black to the darkest part of the shadow.

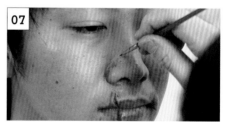

07 Add redness to the wings of the nose and under the lip.

08 Mix Liquitex Quinacridone red-orange, some gel, and some thickening medium to make Liquitex blood. Dissolve with water and apply to produce the desired bloody look.

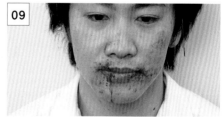

09 Complete. When applying small appliances, limit the use of stage blood because excessive stage blood will actually hide the appliance.

02 | Broken Nose

01 Clean off your model's nose using skin toner. Apply a gelatin appliance using Pros-Aide. When a nose is actually broken its cartilage will bend. However, when applying makeup start the bend *above* the cartilage to produce the look of an obviously broken nose.

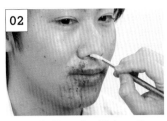

02 Remove flashing using skin toner. Press down on the tip of the nose so the appliance sticks. Move the appliance to either side to increase the angle of the broken nose.

03 Add redness where the nose is bent as you mix acrylic colors (two types of red, burnt brown, purple, black, ocher).

04 Add red lines under the eye and in the middle of the forehead. Smudge the colors.

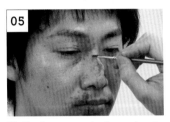

05 Mix Liquitex green and yellow and apply to the outside of the redness to produce the bruised look.

06 Use Liquitex Blood to produce the traces of a nose bleed. Then, smudge off to the side using a finger. Doing this gives the impression of traces from the hands of an attacker.

07 Drop some stage blood on the collar of the shirt in order to represent spattered blood. Be sure to spread blood around so it looks natural.

08 Complete!

03 | Swollen Eye

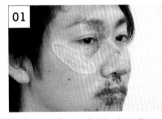

01 Apply an appliance slightly above the cheekbone.

02 Apply Pros-Aide on the eyelid while the eye is closed. Then, apply a gelatin appliance.

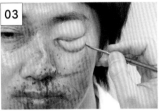

03 Paint red-purple along the line of the swollen eye and under the eye. Then, smudge.

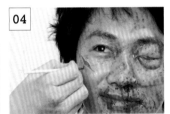

04 Paint orange inside the wound.

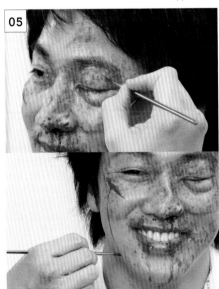

05 Paint amber inside the wound and orange outside the wound. Further, surround the wound in purple. Add eyelash shadows using black. Drop Liquitex blood from the wound and let it drip down the cheek.

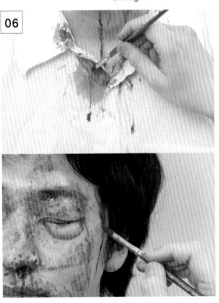

06 Use Liquitex blood to soil the inside of the shirt and the temple.

COMPLETE! At the photo shoot, pour some stage blood in a paper cup and have your model take it in their mouth. Then, let the blood ooze down from the mouth.

Morgue Bride

by Akihito

The concept is a disfigured bride who has been dismembered and then stitched back together. Create silicone, foam latex, and gelatin appliances - apply them to produce the wounds on the neck, chest, and wrist.

Model: Aya, a freelance writer/model

SFX MAKEUP 03

[Materials]
Silicone appliances for the wrist and chest (silicone synthetic skin), gelatin appliance for the arm (gelatin synthetic skin), foam latex for the neck (foam latex synthetic skin), TELESIS (adhesive to glue on silicone synthetic skin), acetone, Liquitex, Pros-Aide, Cabosil mixed Pros-Aide, string, Skin Illustrator, Gel 10, deadener, liquid latex, foundation, water-activated face powder, Reel Color, ethanol, Dura (blue, red, navy), Aeroflash, eyeliner, blonde wig, color contact lenses, false eyelashes, adhesive for false eyelashes and wig

[Tools]
Pins, brushes, airbrush, sponge

01   Attaching the Appliances

01 The neck appliance is made from foam latex. Place it against the neck to verify the size.

02 Apply Pros-Aide and allow to dry. Then attach the appliance to the neck.

03 Join seams together at back of the neck.

04 Use Pros-Aide to smooth out the edges of the appliance, then powder it down.

05 The appliance on the wrist is silicone. The wound on the wrist is made in a ring-shape, so it can be slipped over your model's hand.

06 Glue the appliance on using TELESIS and dissolve away the edges by applying acetone. The wound above the wrist is a gelatin appliance. Glue on with Pros-Aide.

07 Glue some string on the chest appliance using TELESIS. Then, lay the appliance on your model's chest.

08 Apply Pros-Aide on the backside of the silicone appliance and then begin applying to your model.

09 Apply TELESIS along the edges of the silicone, then powder it down.

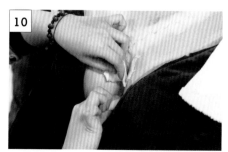

10 Put a silicone appliance on the cleavage. Use TELESIS to attach and powder it down.

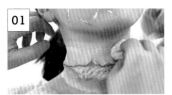

Dab Pros-Aide along the edges of the appliance on the neck.

Apply powder to the wound on the chest.

Mix Gel 10 and deadener together. Dab that on the wounds. Using a sponge, dab a mixture of liquid latex and foundation on the wounds.

Avoiding the wounds, apply water-activated face powder.

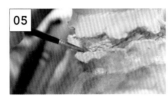

Use ethanol to activate Reel Color. Apply ocher color on the wounds.

Apply dark brown Skin Illustrator inside the wounds.

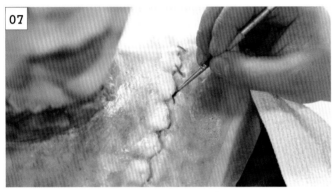

Use black Skin Illustrator to paint stitches on the wounds.

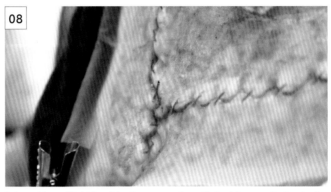

Dab a mixture of Gel 10 and deadener across the entirety of the wounds. Powder it down.

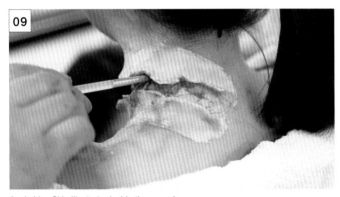

Apply blue Skin Illustrator inside the wounds.

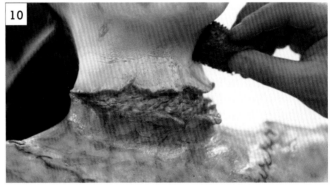

Use an orange stipple sponge to dab on the same blue Skin Illustrator you used in step 09. Airbrush blue Dura to produce veins.

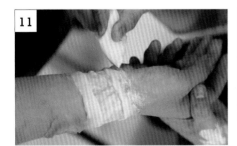

Apply ocher Reel Color on the wrist.

Airbrush navy Dura on the joints of the fingers to make them look dark. Use the same color to draw some veins.

Use an orange stipple sponge to apply yellowish brown Skin Illustrator on the wrist.

14

Use yellow and blue Skin Illustrator to draw sinews. Paint them over using yellow and red.

15

Mix red and blue Dura to create purple, and add that to the darkest areas.

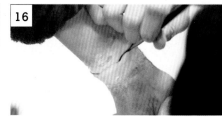

16

Add the same color from step 15 to the wrist.

03 Makeup on the Face

01

Wipe your model's face using makeup remover to clean. Plot out the shape of a wound using eyeliner. The concept here is to replicate small cuts on the face caused by pieces of broken glass.

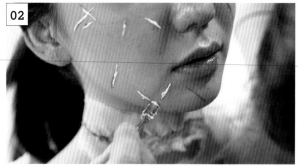

02

Apply Cabosil mixed with Pros-Aide on the plot to produce a weal.

03

Avoid the small cuts while applying water-activated powder on the face.

04

Mix red and brown Skin Illustrator and apply to the cuts.

05

Mix red, yellow and black Aeroflash. Then, airbrush to blend the edges of the wound on the neck.

06

Use a lash adhesive to attach false eyelashes on both the upper and lower eyelashes.

07

Apply black eyeliner and grayish beige eyeshadow.

08

Put gray and brown mixed color contact lenses in each eye. Add a blonde wig.

COMPLETE!

Dress your model with a wedding gown that has a weathered look on both the chest and the underarms to complete.

[Killer] from Killer & Tailor

by Tomo Hyakutake

The concept of Killer & Tailor is that of a slasher and a tailor. The killer cuts her victim's skin off. The tailor sews the pieces of skin on his body as a fish-like scale.

Model: Sayaka Machii

SFX MAKEUP 04

[Materials]
Cabosil mixed Pros-Aide, water-activated powder, grease paint, silicone putty, stage blood, prop scissors, Derma Shield, net, PAX, acrylic paint, Skin Illustrator, Pros-Aide, TELESIS, acetone, color contact lenses (red), wig (red)

[Tools]
Brushes, toothbrush, sponge, spatula, cotton swabs

01 Wounds on the Hands and Legs

01 Apply Cabosil mixed with Pros-Aide on the arms and legs while making scratch-like wounds.

02 Apply water-activated powder on the skin.

03 Paint red-purple grease paint over the scratch-like wounds by dry brushing. Apply powder.

02 Wounds on the Back of the Hand

01 Mix equal parts silicone putty part A and part B. Put the blade of the prop scissors between the fingers.

02 Apply the silicone putty mixture to produce an open wound that splits the base of the fingers.

03 Paint above the open wound using purple from mixing red and blue grease paint.

04 Apply water-activated powder on the skin.

05 Apply stage blood on the palm of the hand to produce a bloody look.

06 Complete!

Makeup on the Face

01

Apply Derma Shield on your model's face. Put a hairnet on the model and apply PAX on the eyebrows to conceal them.

02

Apply Pros-Aide to the backside of the silicone appliance and on the model's forehead.

03

Align between the eyebrows and put the silicone appliance on the cheek.

04

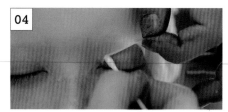

Apply TELESIS on the edge of the silicone to attach. Apply acetone along the edges of the silicone to dissolve away and remove flashing.

05

Apply Cabosil mixed with Pros-Aide to smooth down the edges of the silicone.

06

Apply a mixture of Pros-Aide and acrylic paint to produce a wound.

07

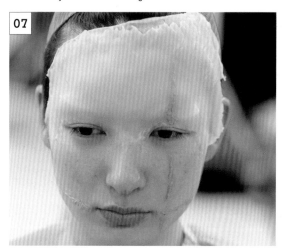

Similarly, produce a wound under the eye. Then, apply powder.

10

Add red-purple grease paint under the eye.

11

Use black to smudge around the eyes, then smudge with brown. Draw a red line under the eye that is not wounded.

08

Splatter red-purple Skin Illustrator using a toothbrush.

09

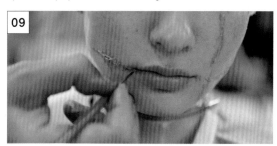

Apply the Pros-Aide and acrylic paint mixture to the corner of the mouth to produce a wound.

COMPLETE!

Add a pair of red color contact lenses and a wig to complete.

[Tailor] from Killer & Tailor

by Tomo Hyakutake

Human skin is actually made up of red snapper scales – that is the idea that conceived this particular character. On one arm, draw a tattoo using COPIC markers.

SFX MAKEUP 05

Model: Tenmetsu, a dancer from the dance company, Ankoku Buto.

---

01 | How to Draw Tattoos using COPIC Markers

[Materials] COPIC marker (black, gray, red, blue)

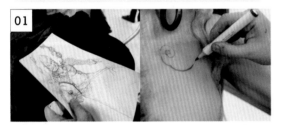

01

Draw a tattoo, using a black COPIC marker, referring to the design sketch.

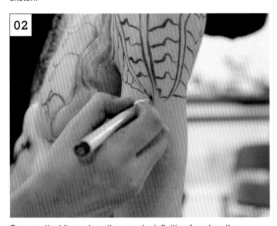

02

Draw vertical lines along the muscle definition found on the shoulder.

03

The shape of the scales influences the finished look. Firmly outline each scale with black lines.

04

Apply gray, one shade lighter than the black, inside the scales while fusing the black outline with the gray. Apply more gray in such a manner that the further away from the black outline you are the paler the gray gets. This will add depth.

05

The black outline has become thin so trace it again.

06

One point for drawing on the chest is to make sure that the right and left sides are symmetrical.

07

Add red, closer to vermillion, to complete underpainting.

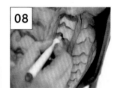

08

At the end, add blue below the outline of the scales in such a matter as to add shadows to complete.

09

Complete!

Makeup on the Face

[Materials] COPIC markers, Gel 10 bald cap, acetone, TELESIS, Dura, Skin Tite®, grease paint, silicone appliance, fangs, false nails, color contact lenses (white)
[Tools] Brushes, toothbrush

The appliance for the skin is made from Smooth-On silicone. Paint stitches on the appliance. As for the red snapper, the face is made from latex and the body is urethane foam.

01

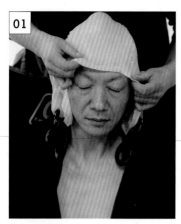

Apply a Gel 10 bald cap on your model's head and glue on using Skin Tite®.

02

Apply the appliance that goes on your model's face and adjust its position. Glue on using TELESIS.

03

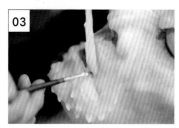

Apply acetone along the edges of the appliance to remove flashing.

04

The photo above shows when the face appliance is in place.

05

Put an appliance, made from Smooth-On silicone, on the body on your model.

06

Use Skin Tite® to glue on the top part first, then work down to the bottom.

07

Apply red, dark brown, and blue Dura mixed color uniformly on the face.

08

Splatter dark brown on the face using a toothbrush.

09

Use Skin Tite® to glue the red snapper prop on the arm.

10

Add a tattoo, using COPIC markers, on the bald cap in a similar manner to the tattoo on the arm.

11

Apply black grease paint around both eyes.

12

Put a white contact lens in each eye.

COMPLETE!

Apply fangs and claw nail tips to complete.

Kogeki

by Tomonobu Iwakura

The concept of this work is an assault, some wounds, and indulging in the use of silicone appliances. The idea of this makeup is self-inflicted wounds with a knife. Eighteen silicone appliances are applied to express the idea of a body covered with wounds. The body piercing is produced using a silicone appliance. Apply a silicone appliance on the forehead and nose to transform your model's face into a westerner. Glue a wig on the bald cap to bring out an edgy feel.

Model: Hiroaki Murakami, who possesses a rock and roll spirit. Regardless of the type of makeup, he always delivers the goods.

[Materials]
Eighteen silicone wound appliances, bald cap, appliances for the forehead and nose, appliances for pointy ears, long bracelet with studs, synthetic skin for body piercing, false nails made of hairpins, casted studs, inexpensive jewelry, fishnet nylons, short pants, organdie skirt, secondhand belt with studs, TELESIS, acetone, Pros-Aide, stage blood, Skin Illustrator, grease paint, false eyelashes, color contact lenses, Cabosil mixed Pros-Aide, nail polish (black), blonde wig

[Tools]
Brushes, airbrush, scissors, orange stipple sponge, blow dryer

01 Makeup for a Wound Covered Body

01 This is an appliance that has fake studs attached. The fake studs were made from a mold cast from a golf tee bought at a dollar store. The studs are secured at the backside of the silicone appliance with wire and surgical tape so that the angle of the studs can be adjusted. Glue on this appliance using TELESIS.

02 Apply TELESIS on your model's skin, then lay down the appliance.

03 Apply a body piercing appliance to the arm.

04 Apply a wound appliance to the neck. Dissolve away the edges of the appliance using acetone. Then, smooth out the edges using Cabosil mixed with Pros-Aide.

05 Apply a stab wound appliance to the side of the torso.

06 Dissolve away the edges of the appliance to remove flashing. After blow drying, powder it down, then apply grease paint using an orange stipple sponge.

07 Prepare a silicone appliance to produce a body piercing. Apply TELESIS on the backside of the appliance. Then, glue to your model's abdomen. Glue it on "the most painful place to pierce."

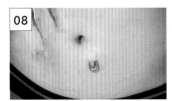

08 Attach an earring to the appliance (this particular one was purchased at Forever 21).

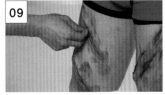

09 Add redness around the wounds using an orange stipple sponge.

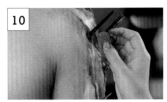

10 Add redness at the base of the studs.

11 Apply stage blood inside the wounds to complete.

Smooth your model's hair using Pros-Aide, then blow dry.

Apply a bald cap whose front is made from latex and back is made from silicone. Glue on using TELESIS beginning with the forehead. Apply TELESIS uniformly at the back of the head and then glue on.

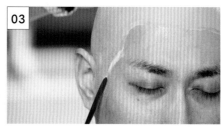

Use acetone to dissolve away the edges of the appliance to remove flashing. Smooth out the edges using Cabosil mixed with Pros-Aide.

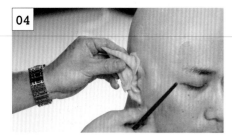

Add pointy ear silicone appliances. Glue on using TELESIS.

Attach an appliance to raise the forehead and add depth to the nose. Adjust the position to make sure it is the middle of the forehead. Glue with TELESIS.

Use acetone to dissolve away the edges of the appliance to remove flashing. Smooth out the edges using Cabosil mixed with Pros-Aide. After blow drying, apply powder.

Cut a blond wig in half. Extend the wig about 2cm (3/4") from the cut edge by sewing on a piece of netting with fishing line, then add hair to the net.

Slide the wig away from the center of the head. Glue on the wig using TELESIS in such a way that the bald area and the wig cover a 3 to 2 ratio area.

For the studs glued on the head, apply five layers of Pros-Aide on the base of each stud. Doing so will allow the layers of Pros-Aide to provide elasticity and prevent the studs from coming off the bald cap. For transport purposes, apply a piece of transparent sticker sheet to the base of each stud after applying the layers of Pros-Aide.

Use Pros-Aide to glue each stud on the silicone bald cap. Do not use TELESIS because it will melt the layers of Pros-Aide on the base of the stud.

Apply Pros-Aide surrounding the area of each stud to reinforce. After blow drying, apply powder.

Apply red Skin Illustrator at the base of each stud.

Airbrush around both eyes using black. Add shadows using black grease paint along the eyeline.

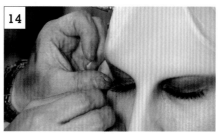

Apply false eyelashes using TELESIS, and then apply another piece of false eyelashes using TELESIS. Applying false eyelashes increase the dramatic look of the eyes.

Add black eyeliner along both lower eyelids to complete.

Tips for Detailing and Finishing Touches

01

After putting on the fishnet nylons, cut them to show off the wounds.

02

Drop stage blood on the shoulder area studs.

03

The shoes are original. Make a heel using FRP and glue it on a pair of purchased vinyl shoes.

04

Attach jewelry for the body piercing.

05

Put on black mesh top.

06

The studs on the long bracelet are lightweight studs cast from a golf tee, so they won't droop due to their weight.

07

Apply black nail polish on the right-hand nails. On the left, attach synthetic nails that are modeled using hair scissors from a dollar store.

08

Glue studs in a cluster on the backs of the hands. Make a mold using a flat head stud and cast the mold to make multiples of the studs. Use TELESIS to glue on.

09

Drop stage blood on all wounds.

10

Splatter dark brown on the face.

COMPLETE!

Apply black on the lips.

Kyuaisha

SFX MAKEUP 07

by Soichi Umezawa

This guy is deeply in love with a girl and he is desperate to have her love him back. To impress her, he tattooed the girl's favorite brand's trademarks on his face. However, it didn't turn out well. Leaving the tattoos on the nose area, which are relatively successful, he applied leather to conceal the other tattoos and completed his transformation. He is just about to confess his love to the girl and express his feelings towards her.

The brand's trademarks are stamped on a silicone appliance using stamps made out of pieces of paper.

Model: Shigeru Okuze, an actor. Acting credits include: *Kirishima, Bukatsu yamerutte yo, Ogon wo daite tobe, Akumu chan.*

[Materials] Pros-Aide, silicone appliance (silicone synthetic skin), TELESIS (adhesive to glue silicone), acetone, Liquitex, powder, green contact lenses, Cabosil mixed with Pros-Aide, Sunpelca® (firm urethane foam), false nails, cardboard, leather
[Tools] Hairpins, brushes, airbrush, orange stipple sponge

01 Trademark Makeup

01 Use hair gel to smooth the back the bangs and secure using hairpins.

02 Apply Pros-Aide on the eyebrows and facial hair to flatten.

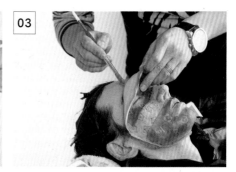

03 Apply powder, then transfer the silicone appliance onto your model's face. Be sure to align with the middle of the forehead.
For the creation of a face cast, please refer to p.86 of *Conceptual Special Effects Makeup 2.*

04 Glue on the appliance using TELESIS, beginning with the forehead.

05 Glue the appliance around the mouth area, covering your model's lips.

06 Glue the appliance on the nose in such a manner that the edges of the appliance touch the inside of the nostrils.

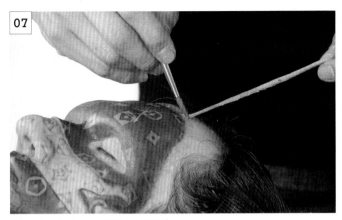

Use acetone to slowly remove the flashing.

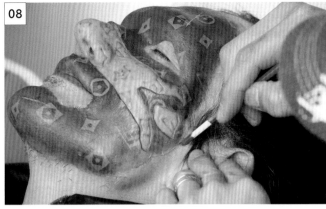

Use the end of a brush to carefully smooth the edges of the appliance to blend in with the skin.

Smooth out the edges of the appliance using Cabosil mixed with Pros-Aide (a mixture of Pros-Aide and Cabosil, glass fiber).

Use brown, red, and black Skin Illustrator to make a color of the leather. Then, airbrush where necessary.

Plug the ear with your finger to prevent airbrushing inside the ear.

Use a brush to paint the nooks and crannies of the ear. To produce textures, mix paint to make a darker brown and then dab on using an orange stipple sponge.

Use a brush to splatter black Skin Illustrator to add textures. Press with powder.

Glue on false nails, with nail polish applied, using TELESIS.

Mix Liquitex brown and ocher to make the color of the trademarks. Make a stamp using a piece of cardboard and Sunpelca®. Then, apply the mixed Liquitex color.

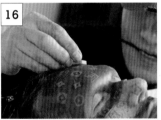

Firmly press the stamp against the appliance. Press down the stamp uniformly with your fingers.

Slowly remove the stamp.

Paint with a brush wherever the stamp is thin, then apply powder.

Paint the trademarks on the skin tone appliance using red.

After putting green contact lenses in each eye, apply face paint around both eyes to complete.
Add desired finishing touches to complete.

How to Make an Appliance, a Stamp, and Dentures

[Materials] Lifecast (plaster) of makeup applicant, NSP clay, silicone texture pad, Leon clay, plaster, Baldiez, Vaseline, Pros-Aide, Gel 10, deadener, Skin Illustrator, leather, cardboard, Liquitex, false nails, lacquer spray (clear), silicone synthetic tooth, Urethane K2K, two-part urethane paint
[Tools] Pins, brushes, airbrush, de-aerator, straps, utility blade, sandpaper, powder

01

On a lifecast (plaster) of your model, sculpt an original model using NSP clay. Apply silicone on the leather surface to make a texture pad. Press the texture pad against the sculpted clay to add details.

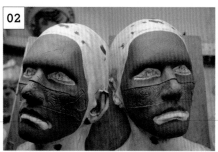

02

The original model is complete.

03

Build flesh using Leon Clay on the edges of the original model.

04

The flesh is complete.

05

❶ Make a mold of the clay sculpted original model using plaster. Once the plaster has cured, remove the clay and sparsely apply vaseline on the surface of the mold for releasing.
❷ Use an airbrush to apply three layers of clear Baldiez uniformly on the mold.
❸ After applying three layers, airbrush leather-color Baldiez exclusively on the forehead and cheek areas that are supposed to be brown.
❹ Finally, airbrush clear Baldiez on the nose area. In order to maintain the fine details of the leather, color the silicone in advance. That way the layers of paint applied on the appliance won't cover the leather texture.

06

After finishing the Baldiez airbrushing, apply Pros-Aide. Apply vaseline on the positive mold as well. After airbrushing Baldiez, apply Pros-Aide.

07

Mix Gel 10 part A, part B, and deadener in 1:1:2.5 ratio. Put the mixture on a de-aerator then pour into the mold. Put the positive mold on and firmly press the mold. Wrap a strap around to secure.

08

❶ Use powder to release the appliance from the mold. Use similarly colored powder when removing the brown part of the appliance.
❷ After releasing the appliance from the mold, paint it using Skin Illustrator. Once the paint has finished, coat the appliance with Baldiez.

09

Design the trademarks for the stamp. Cut pieces of cardboard to make stamps. Stamp the trademarks on the painted appliance using Liquitex.

10

Sand the false nails using sandpaper. Paint the backside of the nails using Liquitex. Spray on clear lacquer to coat the painted nails.

11

Dentures. It wasn't possible to take a dental impression of the model. Instead, a set of soft dentures was made by applying urethane K2K over a silicone dental impression (if the dentures are soft, some degree of adjustment can be made). Paint the dentures using two-part urethane paint. At last, coat the dentures using clear urethane.

Wound Makeup
Contest Entered Works

Film directors Takashi Shimizu, Yoshihiro Nishimura, and Yudai Yamaguchi judged wound makeup submitted for the contest. This section announces the contest results and reviews each work, including first place! The winning makeup can be found on p.24.

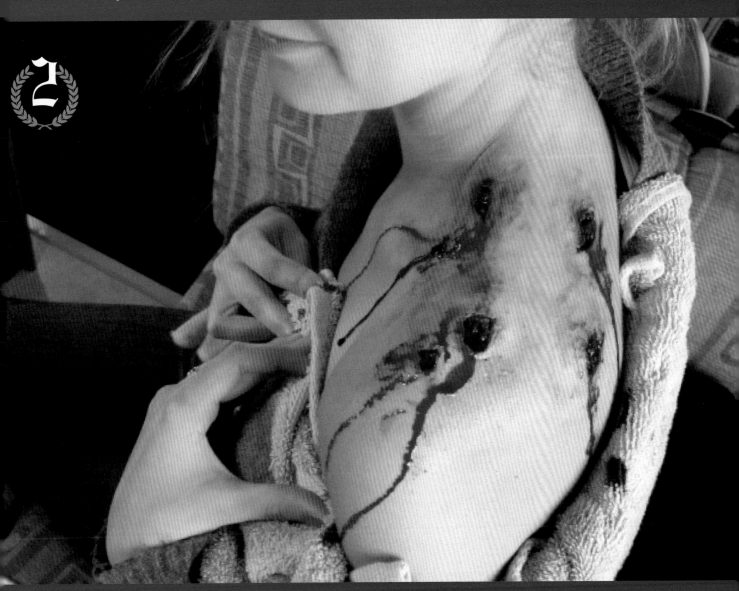

The winning makeup can be found on p.24.

Selected by Yoshihiro Nishimura, Yudai Yamaguchi

Second Place
Dog Bite Wounds

Wakana Yoshihara

Materials: Appliance, Skin Illustrator FX Palette, wound filler, stage blood, vaseline, Pros-Aide
Graduate of/Attending: Mano College of Beauty, London College of Fashion

"I personally liked her submission because she sent in both makeup with blood and without blood. She has already begun working professionally and I think that I can trust her work without worrying too much. There are many materials that meld well with the skin here, so it is a bit difficult to evaluate the entirety of the work. That being said, it is obvious to me that she had a firm grasp on wound makeup principles prior to submitting this work." (Nishimura)

"To put it simply, I think this piece was technically very well done." (Yamaguchi)

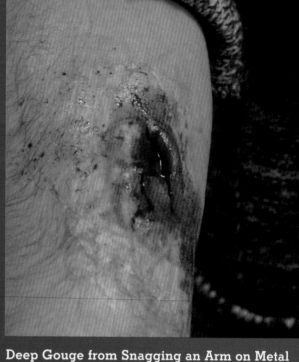

Deep Gouge from Snagging an Arm on Metal
Wakana Yoshihara
Materials: Silicone appliance, Skin Illustrator FX Palette, cotton, stage blood, TELESIS
Graduate of/Attending: Mano College of Beauty, London Collage of Fashion

Selected by Takashi Shimizu
Second Place

Kado (Flower Arrangement)
Rena Manabe
Concept: A new style of flower arrangement
Materials: 3rd Degree, grease paint
Graduate of/Attending: AMAZING SCHOOL JUR

"I have a few concerns with the technical aspects of this work and its unusual style, which comes across as perhaps a bit extreme. However, it proceeds from standard special effects makeup that we regularly see in films, so I find the idea behind it really interesting." (Shimizu)

"I am really fond of this makeup. A flower arrangement attached to the face! I might actually use this makeup in my film. As far as the technical work is concerned, there is room for improvement. But, I can only imagine how difficult it was to hold the weight of those silk flowers." (Nishimura)

"I think that I can do makeup like this myself... although I might have trouble maintaining it for a long time. It's a very interesting idea though." (Yamaguchi)

Corned Beef Girl
Kiyoka Suzuki, Shizuka Imanari, Yuta Yamaguchi
Concept: This wound was created while thinking of something delicious.
Materials: Wax, can of corned beef
Graduate of/Attending: Tokyo Visual Arts College

"The model is more impactful than the makeup itself. She is really cute. I think it was a great choice to apply this makeup to such a cute girl." (Yamaguchi)

"I like this submission." (Nishimura)

Face that has been Punched Repeatedly
Wakana Yoshihara
Materials: Silicone appliances (around the eyes), Skin Illustrator FX Palette, Skin Illustrator, Pros-Aide, Top Guard Skin Barrier, stage blood, wound filler, silicone putty, tissue paper
Graduate of/Attending: Mano College of Beauty, London Collage of Fashion

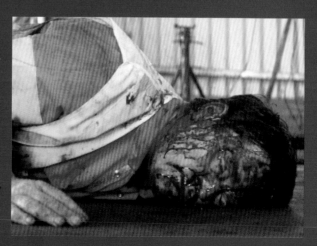

Third Place

Setsudan Illusion (Detachment Illusion)

Jun Agata

Concept: A body cutting magic trick is the idea for this self-makeup. It is supposed to represent a magic trick, so I didn't use stage blood. I didn't want to make it too grotesque. Apply makeup to the silicone appliances to produce the uneven torso. Conceal the model's belly button and make a fake one using silicone in order to shift the torso's centerline. Add a skull-shaped tattoo to enhance the look of the shifted torso and then glue on some hair to complete.

Materials: Gel 10 (wound, concealing a belly button, fake belly button), hair, tattoo sheet

Graduate of/Attending: Tokyo Visual Arts College

"From the submitted photo I am not sure that this makeup would be acceptable for closeups. However, I think that the concept behind it is quite good. The small amount of deception is actually a surprising element of this makeup. The belly button is concealed, and hair is added to the chest – this is subtle but effective, I think. I also think that adding some stage blood will enhance the overall look." (Nishimura)

"The position of the lower half of the skull and the shift of the lower torso could be a bit better. However, if you look closely you will think to yourself, "Oh, I get it!" Better composition of the submission photo would have helped the overall look I think." (Shimizu)

"I admit that this makeup uses a lot of interesting tricks. However, the quality of submission photo is seriously lacking. Sadly, it's out of focus! Something could have easily been done to improve the situation – perhaps using a reddish background, given that the theme here is a magic trick?" (Yamaguchi)

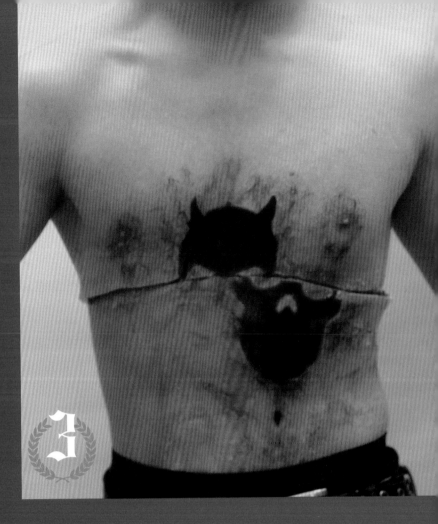

collection

Mari Seki

Concept: A stitched up marionette

Materials: Pros-Aide, Cabosil, paint, thread

Graduate of/Attending: Tokyo University of Arts Department of Intermedia Art

"I like this one." (Nishimura)

"Unless someone told you, I think it might be hard to see this as a marionette. This is the pose before the marionette has been manipulated." (Yamaguchi)

Third Place

See No Evil, Hear No Evil, Speak No Evil

Miyuki Tahara

Concept: Intentionally creating a monkey that embodies the idea of "See no evil, hear no evil, speak no evil." Stitching up the wounds up shows the enhanced intention behind this work.

Materials: Foam rubber, PAX, grease paint, feather boa

Graduate of/Attending: Atelier Allure

"The idea behind this is super interesting. Forcing the concept of "see no evil, hear no evil, speak no evil" on a monkey is interesting and I think the technical aspects are quite good also. I see skills outside of the wound makeup application itself. I would definitely offer her work if I have any in the future." (Yamaguchi)

"I really liked this submission, although I don't really consider it to be true wound makeup. That is why I didn't choose it for the first place prize. I think this is more or less a mask." (Nishimura)

STARDUST
Sachi Yanagida

Concept: The flowing blood is in the form of galactic stardust. In addition, glitter is mixed in with the stage blood as a sign of incorporating fashion.
Materials: Pros-Aide, Cabosil, Silicone KE-12, NSP clay, clear lacquer spray, rubber tube, glitter, stage blood, nail polish, wig
Graduate of/Attending: Tokyo Visual Arts College

"I think this makeup took a long time to produce. I like it." (Nishimura)

"I think that if this makeup were applied to the whole body, or at least down to the buttocks, it would look amazing. I have seen similar makeup on the upper body before. Even "Body World" exhibits have well thought out poses and originality, so I think this work needed something more. This is a contest after all. I felt that there was an assumption that just applying makeup to the upper body was enough. Moreover, if it weren't stated, the glitter wouldn't be noticeable." (Yamaguchi)

Tribal Scarification Makeup
Yuka Watanabe

Concept: A Maori tribal tattoo is the inspiration for this artistic wound makeup.
Materials: 3rd Degree, grease paint, stage blood
Graduate of/Attending: AMAZING SCHOOL JUR School

"If this makeup showed up on a film location, it would be no problem at all to shoot." (Yamaguchi)

Scarification
Hiroshi Furusho

Concept: This makeup expresses a self-inflicted scarification wound. It's a type of body art - like a tattoo. It is basically a stylized capital letter H.
Materials: NSP clay, naphtha, baby powder, Pros-Aide, Cabosil, grease paint, flocking, silicone, plastic paper, tattoo paper, water, Skin Illustrator, translucent powder, stage blood
Graduate of/Attending: AKIHITO Make-up Private School

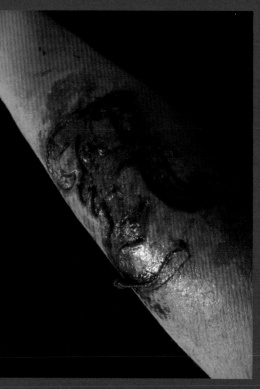

"It is skillful, but looks a bit shiny. In my opinion, the natural hair on the arm and the area where the makeup is applied isn't blended well. If it were blended well, it would definitely impress me more." (Yamaguchi)

"The tattoo successfully expresses the idea of a wound. The application of the stage blood is on point and I give it high praise. I just wish the letter were more elaborate." (Nishimura)

He has so-called "salmon machismo." He is infatuated with his abs, but no matter how he tries he can't get a six-pack. So, he sliced his abs to create his own six-pack.
Shigeyuki Sasano

Concept: A muscular man, with the body of a salmon, has forcibly sliced his abs in a desperate attempt to have six-pack abs.
Materials: Latex rubber, acrylic paint, clear paint, airbrush paint
Graduate of/Attending: Tokyo Visual Arts College

"I think this piece would have been more interesting if it was more realistic. When you make a salmon, you should make it more shiny! This doesn't look delicious at all. By the way, is there such a thing as 'salmon machismo?'" (Yamaguchi)

"This isn't wound makeup as much as it is modeling." (Nishimura)

Jonbi
Chiharu Mutsuda

Concept: This makeup is produced by focusing on a grotesque appearance that can only be achieved with prosthetic makeup. Particular focus was given to the rendering of split flesh around the mouth and the creation of a certain dental texture.
Materials: Foam rubber, PAX, grease paint, stage blood
Graduate of/Attending: Atelier Allure

"It looks like a zombie from a 1970's Italian film. I would recommend studying more current zombie makeup. Also, I think the teeth could have been better. It is best to create this type of makeup in such a way that it tells us how the zombie died. Remember that a zombie isn't technically a monster. George Romero zombies and Lucio Fulci zombies are totally different. If you are a zombie lover, I think you should add elements that express your obsession with zombies into your makeup." (Yamaguchi)

Humanoid
Yayoi Sakuma

Concept: Steampunk
Materials: 3rd Degree, bicycle parts
Graduate of/Attending: AMAZING SCHOOL JUR School

"I want this work to show more love for Steampunk." (Yamaguchi)

Self-operation
Masami Sato (Studio BAKESHI)

Concept: Performing an operation on oneself sometime in the near future
Materials: Foam latex, plastic
Graduate of/Attending: Tokyo Visual Arts College

"At first, I thought he was a DJ. I think the muscle should have a more fleshy look. The face expresses pain, even though there shouldn't be any pain when the wound looks dry like this. Right?" (Yamaguchi)

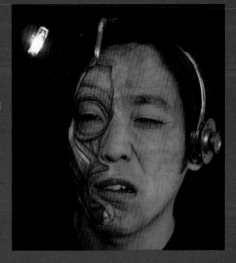

Ooops!
Ayaka Funaba
Profile not available

"This sort of theme is nothing new. Too much stage blood hides the nail on the injured finger though, so the realism is diminished. I wish this submission was a little more over the top. For example, if half a finger was ground up in a mortar or shredded by a peeler of some kind." (Yamaguchi)

Brainbuster
Makoto Hibino

Concept: An alien has jumped out of a body and there is a large rupture wound in the stomach.
Materials: Foam latex
Graduate of/Attending: Tokyo Film Center Eiga Haiyu Senmongakko

"Don't you think it would be better to show the alien? As far as the technical aspects are concerned this makeup could be used as a dummy, but it has no nipples!" (Nishimura)

"The title says 'Brainbuster,' but there is no 'brain.' I would suggest working on the human anatomy first. I do not agree with the idea that simply messing with internal organs passes as wound makeup. One more thing, the way that the cloth covers the body should have been done better." (Yamaguchi)

Ningen Shokuzai
Kanna Nakano

Concept: A newlywed wife who enjoys cooking using body parts.
Materials: Wax, silicone putty, polyester resin
Graduate of/Attending: AMAZING SCHOOL JUR School

"The coloring on the fingers doesn't match! The idea of simply cutting off some fingers using a knife is so cliché that it should not be an idea for wound makeup anymore. The artist should go further, like making sushi using the dismembered fingers or at least adding some human fingered sushi beside the hand. This submission needs a little more ingenuity." (Nishimura)

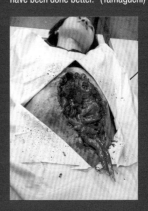

Nishimura and Yamaguchi Talk About Wound Makeup

Wound Makeup Contest

Wound Makeup Contest Entries

Reviews by film director, Yudai Yamaguchi, Yoshihiro Yamaguchi, Takashi Shimizu

The first wound makeup contest invited three remarkable film directors who love special effects makeup, wound makeup, and horror makeup. The first place winner, by unanimous decision, was *Ningyo* by Chie Ichigaya! (p.24) This section introduces the reviewing and judging processes used by Yudai Yamaguchi and Yoshihiro Nishimura, as well as comments from Takashi Shimizu.

Takashi Shimizu Judging Criterion

First of all, does the photo submission stir my imagination? Can I imagine a certain worldview or story from my initial impression? How visually enticing is the work, what is the idea behind it, and what is its creative power? This formed the basis of my selections. I left the technical judging and details to Nishimura and Yamaguchi.

Nishimura: Thank you all for the enthusiastic submissions we received. Each one was packed with fresh ideas and they were all excellent works in their own right. I believe that wound makeup is frequently shot in close-up, so if your goal is to work as a professional makeup artist always ask yourself, "Does this stand the test when shot in close-up?" This idea always comes first on my list of judging criteria, although I must admit that I cover things up with stage blood when I don't have time. This is a very useful way to save time when on location. However, for this contest, I assumed that everyone had plenty of time and carried out their process at their own pace. One critical example is the "Tribal Scarification Makeup." You might be wondering why I didn't choose this one, despite its relative level of skill? All I can say is, when you don't have a restricted time frame and you are a skilled artist, please be a little more diligent! Maybe that is too critical of course…(laugh).

Yamaguchi: This isn't daring enough. The work must produce a strong enough impression to make us think, "Oh, I see what you were trying to do there!" Honestly, makeup should be understood just by looking at a photo. No explanation necessary.

Editor: First place artist Ichigaya and second place artist Yoshihara both created realistic makeup. What were the differences between the two of them?

Nishimura: Yoshihara, the second place winner, is as skilled as a professional. For example, how she created the insides of the bloodless wounds. This shows the level of her skill, even though I personally wanted to see a bit more there. First place winner Ichigaya's photo composition and photo color tones scored quite high. So did the cotton balls on the wound. All of these things may not have been planned, but sometimes things that happen by chance can play an import role in life.

Yamaguchi: The quality of the submission photo is very crucial. In this regard, works awarded first place almost always have very high quality photos. The second place submission photo looks like it was taken in a makeup room. Since this is for a contest, I think that Yoshihara should have done something about that photo. In that respect, the work of Ichigaya is far better.

Editor: When working on a project — if a realistic wound is requested — is it better to make a realistic wound that is easy to see?

Nishimura: It totally depends on the director. For blood, one director — Sion Sono — prefers brown whereas I prefer light red. When realism is sought, use brownish blood. Use red blood when you want to make things showy and visually stimulating.

Yamaguchi: I prefer unrealistic wound makeup. In low budget horror films in the 80s, it was obvious when decapitated prop heads went flying. I like to enjoy horror films, even when I notice those things, like "Oh, they switched to a prop head!" However, as far as wound makeup is concerned, I think it should show how the human skin blends with the prosthetic skin. In this regard, wound makeup requires the greatest technical expertise. Without it, wound makeup will never be successful.

Nishimura: In review, I just want to say to everyone, "Let's go overboard!" Being told by someone that they have seen this exact kind of makeup before is obviously not a compliment.

Yamaguchi: For example, the dismembered fingers submissions. There are many other items in a kitchen besides knives. Also, both used carrots as a prop.

Nishimura: Maybe they were on sale! (laugh)

Yamaguchi: For other submissions, I feel like I have seen similar concepts before. Also, some of the submissions had makeup themes and submission photos that didn't match. With the zombie makeup, I didn't actually feel that there was an obsession with zombies. There was a slight undertone where the intention of that work was just to create generalized, vague images of a zombie as a monster. It lacked depth, I think. For the steampunk theme, I wanted more love of steampunk expressed within the work. I feel like if we were to say, "This isn't steampunk!" this person would simply give up on the steampunk style. I just didn't feel much passion there.

Nishimura: Whether you can be a professional or not depends on whether you are capable of exposing your obsession or not.

Yamaguchi: In my opinion, if this person created something very special, even if it didn't match the objectives of this contest exactly, I surely would remember the contestant as a person who created an awesome steampunk-style work. If I have the chance to work on a project with a steampunk theme, I would certainly ask this person to join the project. I think we are simply questioning passion here.

Nishimura: In general, I would say that most the submissions did not go overboard. It is possible for the contestants to do so.

Yamaguchi: Being told somebody else can do your job would be the end of your career. This applies to film directing as well. In this regard, I feel that there is something novel in See No Evil, Hear No Evil, Speak No Evil. It seems like this contestant would have the answer if I said, "I am seeking some good new ideas."

Takashi Shimizu

Film director. Born in 1972 in Gunma prefecture. After working as a property master and an assistant director, Shimizu debuted as a director in a three minute TV drama. His *Ju-On* series was a great success. He worked on V-Cinema and a feature film version of *Ju-On* as well as *The Grudge* franchise in Hollywood. Film credits include: *Marebito* (2004), *Reincarnation* (2005), *Tormented* (2011) and many others. He worked with Yudai Yamaguchi on the TV drama *The Great Horror Family* (2004) and *Soil* (2010). He has had frequent cameo appearances in Nishimura's films as a mysterious Chinese man. Currently, Shimizu is in pre-production on a fantasy film that has a completely different air from his horror films.

Yudai Yamaguchi

Film director. Born in 1971 in Tokyo prefecture. Yamaguchi's film, *Battlefield Baseball*, won the Grand Prize in the youth competition category at the Yubari International Fantastic Film Festival in 2002. Yamaguchi's film credits include: *Cromatie High - The Movie* (2004), *Yakuza Weapon* (2010) as co-director with Taku Sakaguchi, and many others. Yamaguchi co-directed the TV drama *Soil* with Takashi Shimizu in 2010.

Yoshihiro Nishimura

Film director, special effects makeup creator, modeling, and gore effects. Born in 1967 in Tokyo prefecture. Nishimura got enormous support from fantastic film festivals all around the world and he presented a brand new category called "gore effects." Nishimura's film credits include: *Tokyo Gore Police* (2008), *Mutant Girls Squad* (2010), *Helldriver* (2010), and many others.

First place: Cash prize JAP¥100,000. Second and Third place: Stage blood, silicone putty, and other merchandise.

Author Profiles

AKIHITO

Born in Fukuoka prefecture, Akihito is the chief of Shiniseya Fine Arts Studio. He is three-time consecutive champion of the special effects makeup episodes for the Japanese television program "TV Champion." He is the only Japanese artist to win the prestigious IMATS Avant-Garde makeup competition, where top notch makeup artists gather from around the world. Akihito moved to the United States in 2002 and is currently working at a special effects makeup studio in Los Angeles as the key-artist. He has shown us his particular world-view in the fine arts field and was named recipient of the silver award for his work Heart of Art in the notoriously difficult FineArt Book SPECTRUM 15 3D section. Similarly, in SPECTRUM 16, his work "Elegant Medusa" received the gold award. His film credits include: *Alien vs Predator*, *The Chronicles of Narnia*, *Alice in Wonderland*, *Iron Man 2*, *The Revenant*, *Terminator Salvation*, *Terminator Genisys*, *Guardians of the Galaxy Vol.2*, *Deadpool 2*, *Robot 2.0* and more.

Akiteru Nakada

Born in Saitama prefecture. He met his mentor, Kazuhiro Tsuji, at Yoyogi Animation Gakuin in the SFX Special Visual Effects program. After a stint as Tsuji's assistant, Nakada went independent. After working on various projects in 2012, Nakada started ZOMBIE STOCK Inc. Ever since he was very young, Nakada has been intrigued by all things scary. He received a real shock watching things like *Jaws* and *Dawn of The Dead*. Later, watching the music video Making Michael Jackson's *Thriller* and the documentary film about Tom Savini, *Master of Horror Effects* (produced by Fangoria magazine), greatly influenced his decision to pursue special effects makeup as a profession. His list of credits includes: *Sekigahara*, *Too Young to Die! Wakakushite Shinu*, *The Fable*, *Kuru*, and many others. He also undertakes theater/advertisement art productions such as the Gekidan – Shinkansen theater program and theater programs directed by Yukio Ninagawa.

Kakusei Fujiwara

Born in Kyoto prefecture. Fujiwara was massively influenced by an array of films from various genres that are considered borderless. Influenced by Smith Baker, Borden, and Savini in their prime, Fujiwara decided to pursue the world of special effects makeup. Fujiwara is self-taught and he has truly mastered the techniques of special effects makeup and sculpting. After working at representative studios in Japan (Egawa, Wakasa, Haraguchi), he became independent and founded "Dummy Head Designs." With special effects makeup/dummy making as the basis of his studio, he is actively involved in various media such as films, commercials, etc., while undertaking character design, maquette making, costume making, animatronics, and producing real mannequins. His favorite special effects make-up artist is Giannetto De Rossi from Italy. His films credits include, *Zatoichi*, *SPL Ookami yo Shizukani Shine* (Hong Kong), *K-20 Kaijin Nijumenso-den*, *Eien no Zero*, *KILLERS*, *Flash Point*, *Parasyte: Part 1*, *I am a Hero*, *Ghost in the Shell*, *Inuyashiki*, *The Blood of Wolves*, *Kingdom*, and more.

Makiko Kono

Born in Fukuoka prefecture. In 2004, Kono went to study in England. While she was studying at the University of Hertfordshire as a Modeling & Special Effects major, she took part in many TV programs, films, commercials, special art productions for theater, and costume production projects like props, suits of armor, etc. After graduating, she freelanced and worked as a model maker in London. Since 2011, she has been based in Tokyo. She was influenced by productions like *Alice in Wonderland* (TV movie), *Never Ending Story* (film), and *The Wizard of Oz* (film). Her credits include *Kaizoku to yobareta otoko* (film), *Destiny: Kamakura Monogatari* (film), and more.

Soichi Umezawa

Born in Kanagawa prefecture, Umezawa became interested in film and special effects makeup after watching *The Fury*, *The Howling*, and *Scanners* when he was in junior high. At age sixteen, he decided to pursue the world of special effects makeup in earnest. After graduating high school, through a recommendation from Rick Baker – with whom Umezawa was in contact at the time – he began freelance work at a studio in Japan. He became independent in 1997. Currently, he is a chief of Soichium Inc. His credited films include: *Tenshu Monogatari*, *Koko no Mesu*, *CUT*, *Yokai Ningen Bemu*, *Kirishima bukatsu yamerutteyo* etc. In 2014, Umezawa made his directorial debut in an American short film called *Y is for Youth*, which is part of ABC's *Death 2*. He has subsequently released other short films. In 2017, he released his first feature film *Vampire Clay* in which he undertook the direction, screenplay writing, editing, and special effects makeup.

Tomo Hyakutake

While in high school, Hyakutake studied under Screaming Mad-George. After graduating, he moved to Tokyo and studied under Takeo Kimura at the Nikkatsu Eiga Geijutsu Gakuin and then moved on to study special effects makeup under Kazuhiro Tsuji at Yoyogi Animation Gakuin. He is chief of Hyakutake Studio Inc. He produces special costumes for films, TV series, music videos, and events. He also produces special effects makeup, special models, and character designs. His credited works include: *Dororo*, *CASSHERN*, *Resident Evil: Damnation* (character design), *Museum*, *Earthquake Bird*, *Shin Godzilla*, *Touken Ranbu* (film), *Tokyo Ghoul*, *Tokyo Ghoul S*, *Takizawa Kabuki*, and many more.

Tomonobu Iwakura

Born in Kagawa prefecture. After graduating from Tokyo Visual Arts in 2004 – with a Special Effects Makeup major – Iwakura was involved in various productions as a freelancer. At a very young age, Iwakura was fond of woodworking, crafting, and the manufacturing of objects. His influence is XJAPAN. He has consecutive Kawasaki Halloween Award titles: second place in 2003, first place in 2004, second place in 2005, best group award in 2006, and judge's special award in 2007. Also, he won second place in the 2004 Velfarre Roppongi halloween costume contest, as well as the Ageha Halloween contest in 2010. His credited works include: *The Great Yokai War*, *GeGeGe no Kitaro*, *The Movie Kaibutsu-kun*, *VAMPS HALLOWEEN PARTY LIVE*, *X JAPAN hide MUSEUM2013*, etc.

Yoshinari Dohi

Born in Tokyo. Dohi works in special effects makeup, props, and set design for film. He enjoys creating illustrations for fun. From 2017 to 2019, he won consecutive technical awards at The Pink Grand Prix – a festival of erotica films. In 2019, he was awarded beste genreproduktion at japan-filmfest held in Hamburg. Dohi says that he is a starving modeling artist who continues to get involved in low budget horror films, erotica films, and independent films that are rarely publicized and are impossible to even get to blu-ray. Therefore it is most unlikely anyone will watch the films that Dohi works on. He is on Instagram.

A Complete Guide to Special Effects Makeup 3
Realistic Scar Makeups
by Tokyo SFX Makeup Workshop
ISBN: 9781789094183

Published by Titan Books
A division of Titan Publishing Group Ltd.
144 Southwark Street
London
SE1 0UP

First Titan edition: March 2020
10 9 8 7 6 5 4 3 2

This book was first designed and published in Japan in 2013 by Graphic-sha Publishing
Co., Ltd. This English edition was published in 2020 by Titan Books, a division of
Titan Publishing Group Ltd.

Planning and editing:	Sahoko Hyakutake
Original layout and cover design:	Mitsugu Mizobata
Original layout design:	Naruomi Ichio
File management and illustration:	Rino Ogawa (Aterir Kochi)
Editing:	Maya Iwakawa
Proofreading:	Yuko Sasaki
English edition layout:	Shinichi Ishioka
English translation:	Kevin Wilson
English proofreading:	Simon Ward (Titan Books)
Production and management:	Kumiko Sakamoto (Graphic-Sha Publishing Co., Ltd.)

Did you enjoy this book? We love to hear from our readers. Please email us at
readerfeedback@titanemail.com or write to us at Reader Feedback at the above address.

To receive advance information, news, competitions, and exclusive offers online, please
sign up for the Titan newsletter on our website: www.titanbooks.com

A CIP catalogue record for this title is available from the British Library.

Printed and bound in China.